FOR JUNE

WITH BEST WISHES

Taylor Caldwell

JULY 1990

MAMMOTH GOLD

MAMMOTH GOLD

The Ghost Towns of Lake District

By Gary Caldwell
Edited by Genny Smith

Genny Smith Books
Mammoth Lakes, California

Published by Genny Smith Books, Mammoth Lakes, California
Send winter correspondence (October through May) to:
1304 Pitman Avenue, Palo Alto, California 94301

Library of Congress Cataloging in Publication Data
Caldwell, Gary, 1943–
        Mammoth gold: the ghost towns of Lake District / by Gary Caldwell; Genny Smith, editor.
        Includes bibliographical references.
        ISBN 0–931378–12–5
        1. Mammoth Lakes Region (Calif.)—History. 2. Gold mines and mining—California—Mammoth Lakes Region—History. 3. Cities and towns, ruined, extinct, etc.—California—Mammoth Lakes Region.
        I. Smith, Genny Schumacher.   II. Title.
        F869.M275C35 1990   979.4'48—dc20   89–26340

Cover: If you have ever looked across Lake Mary at Red Mountain in the late afternoon, you will recognize the colors chosen for *Mammoth Gold's* cover. Cover design: Mary Ford

Book Design: David Mike Hamilton

Photographs taken by Gary Caldwell between 1986 and 1988 (unless otherwise attributed)

First printing July 1990

Printed in the United States of America

Dedicated to the memory of my father,
Harold Caldwell, the first outdoorsman of my life

❧ V ❧

CONTENTS

A ROAD FROM WHICH I'VE NEVER TURNED BACK

As a small boy vacationing at Crystal Crag Lodge on Lake Mary, I remember being kept awake by the ball-crusher that clanked and growled all night long, crushing the day's ore from the Monte Cristo Mine on Red Mountain. A few years later, after the mine had shut down, my father and I would wander among the empty buildings and climb around the abandoned machinery, including the ball-crusher. We would make frequent expeditions down Old Mammoth Road to the old mines. Those were glorious adventures—clambering up the dumps, peering into the tunnels (most of them were open then), picking up wood with square nails in it and collecting bits of burned and melted colored glass. Little did I realize then that I had started down a road from which I've never turned back.

When in the fall I would show my treasures to my grandfather, he seemed to be looking at something far away as he caressed the old wood and fingered the square nails. I knew the date those old mines had opened (that was about all I knew) and I knew that was the very year he was born, 1878. But how did he know so much about wood and nails like this, I wondered. Then he brought out a box of old blue photographs and began rummaging through them.

There, that was the one he wanted—a picture of some men sitting on the edge of a railroad flatcar, posing for this picture as they began their shift in the Comstock Mine at Virginia City. And there was grandfather, wiry and muscular, a young man in his early twenties. O yes, as a carpenter he knew all about my wood and square nails, and timbering and shoring and so much more that my head couldn't take it all in, for he had worked in a mine similar to Mammoth's. I was so excited and proud I could have burst. I reveled in discovering that my summer adventures were a direct link to my grandfather's early life and to a time and a place I could never know.

The mining history of Old Mammoth started to consume more and more of my summers as well as my thoughts. When I found a piece of glass or crockery, I wanted to know about the people who used it. Who were they, what kind of work did they do? Did they have children? Were they happy? What did they do for fun? And along with their joys I wanted to know their sorrows.

An older friend, who said she had something to show me, first took me to the pioneer cemetery in the early 1960s. I couldn't believe it. Some remnants of picket fences remained, though most everything else had disappeared, including the wooden grave markers. When I went to the cemetery by myself a few days later, I spent the entire day there—and sat down in the middle of it and cried unashamedly. I have never known another place of such magnificent solitude and peaceful grandeur. And it grieves me beyond words that this very place is slated for development. At the time all I could think of was Elizabeth Allen's poem "Endurance."

Behold, we live through all things—famine, thirst,
    Bereavement, pain; all grief and misery,
All woe and sorrow; life inflicts its worst
    On soul and body—but we cannot die.
Though we be sick, and tired, and faint, and worn—
    Lo, all things can be borne!

A good many years later, with college completed, I needed to submit a thesis topic to my graduate advisor, Dr. John Haskell Kemble of Pomona College, Claremont Graduate School. The day I told him "Mammoth City," my formal study of the mining era's history was under way. That was during 1964–65. In 1981 some excerpts from my master's thesis were published as a booklet by Alan Hensher—Books. This 1990 *Mammoth Gold* is a new, greatly expanded version in book form.

As you read these stories of Mammoth's gold, you may notice some odd and inconsistent spellings and some strange punctuation in the excerpts from old newspapers. No, these are not errors. I have copied them exactly as they were written. You will also notice a few words and phrases that mean nothing to us today; *miners' slang* I call it. You will just have to guess their meanings, as I have had to.

Why have I continued to study and write about these mining camps that have all but vanished? Out of love. Love for a time and a place, love for my grandfather who found such joy in the bits of wood and glass I brought him. Love of the countless hours spent tracking down pieces of the puzzle. Love of the days that turned into weeks and months of hiking and climbing over every inch of the old mining area. Most of all, perhaps, out of love and respect for the men, women and children who lived and worked here and for those who died here. And because my study of the mining days has been such a wonderful adventure and given me so much joy, I feel compelled, in turn, to pass along their fascinating stories to others.

Why did it take so long? Because in one sense historical study is never finished. New discoveries are never-ending and more can always be added. But finally I had to say, "stop." So, for the moment, I've stopped—with a folder titled "More Stuff" already beginning to fill.

Acknowledgments

My deepest appreciation to the staff members of the U. S. Forest Service at Mammoth Lakes for their unstinting cooperation and assistance during the past twenty-five years; little did they realize what the consequences would be when they first let me into their historical files. My appreciation also to staff members of: the Bureau of Land Management and California State Library, both in Sacramento; the U.S. Geological Survey, Menlo Park; the National Archives; the University of California at Los Angeles; the research staff of the Huntington Library; and the Laws Railroad Museum.

The following people have been particularly helpful, patient and tolerant of the neophyte who, beginning years ago, sought entrance to their particular area of expertise with little more than a phone number and a list of questions. They provided information, insights and details and also helped ensure accuracy. My special thanks to all of them, especially to those who trusted me with their knowledge of special places that are fragile or vulnerable; as they will see, their secrets are still secret. The late A. E. Beauregard of Bishop, mining authority, assayer, late owner of several of the original Mammoth claims and co-discoverer (with Billy Vaughn) of the Pine Creek Mine north of Bishop, which for a time was the largest tungsten producer in the world—for providing many key documents; Don Beauregard, son of A. E., Vice-President of the Mammoth Lakes Mining Corporation, who has forgotten more about hard-rock mining than most people will ever know—but was kind enough to share it all, even the stuff he'd forgotten. Richard C. Datin, who discovered "The Mammoth Swindle" in the 23 April 1881 Candelaria *True Fissure;* Bob Dinsmore of Bishop, for his timely information on J. L. C. Sherwin's toll road; the late Verner Johnson, Mammoth visitor from 1919 to the late '30s, experienced with teams and wagons, who opened my eyes to the special characteristics of wagon roads; Raymie Muzquiz, who sandwiched drawing the maps between his professional work as storyboard artist and assistant director. C. Dean Rinehart, U.S.G.S., for clarifying Mineral Hill's geologic history; Mary and Lou Roeser of Sierra Meadows and the Mammoth Lakes Pack Outfit, for insights into the early packing history of Mammoth and for identifying the location of some early pack outfits; Genny Smith, for her patience awaiting this manuscript and for a superb job of editing and publishing; Jack T. Stallman, retired senior civil engineer, U.S. Air Force, for his insights and observations on the wagon road up Sherwin Grade. Bob Tanner of Reds Meadow Pack Station, for determining the location of the South Fork referred to by Franklin Buck; Milt Trimble, artist, graphic designer and Mammoth cabin owner, for his drawing of an arrastre; Chip Van Nattan, Mammoth artist, for loaning old newspapers; Bettie Willard, daughter of Beatrice and Stephen, for permission to use portions of the Stephen H. Willard photograph collection; and the Bancroft Library, University of California, Berkeley, for providing reproductions of the mining camp newspapers.

And to my daughter Sierra, a special and loving acknowledgment: without your help this book could never have been written. Those many mornings at Mammoth when you slept in, during the summers of 1987 and 1988, made this work possible.

Gary Caldwell
Mammoth Lakes, California
June, 1990

The Setting ও

GHOST TOWNS OF LAKE DISTRICT, MONO COUNTY, EASTERN CALIFORNIA

East of the Sierra Nevada lies an arid land totally unlike western California. Its rainfall is low, its streams small, its forests sparse, its air dry and clear, its summers long and hot, its winters long and freezing. This high desert land stretches from the base of the Sierra far to the east, across all of Nevada and half of Utah. Stopping Pacific rain clouds from watering this thirsty region stands the mighty wall of the Sierra Nevada.

During 1877 in this harsh, nameless land, high on the Sierra's eastern slope, eager prospectors staked claims and organized Lake District. Its camps lay at altitudes close to 9,000 feet; surrounding ridges rise more than 2,000 feet higher. In the photograph opposite, the view is northeast from the Sierra crest toward Nevada. Mineral Hill—the center of the mining excitement—is the ridge with the bare, sweeping talus slopes on the right-hand edge of the photograph. Trees surround Lake Mary, at its base. On the left rises bald Pumice (Mammoth) Mountain. Crystal Crag is the steepsided peak, center.

© Stephen H. Willard

MAMMOTH LAKES, LAKE DISTRICT & MAMMOTH MINES

East of California's Central Valley stands the massive Sierra Nevada—nearly 400 miles long, 50 to 80 miles wide and rising from sea level to over 14,000 feet. This gigantic mountain range blocks Pacific rain clouds from reaching the lands to the east; and during the West's early history the Sierra also effectively blocked the explorers and pioneers. Eastern California was the last portion of the state to be explored and settled. On the west the rugged Sierra, to the east desert mountain ranges almost as high, to the north and south miles and miles of parched sand and sagebrush—forbidding mountains and desert long conspired to keep white men out. But the lure of gold and silver finally overcame all foreboding.

Today you can so easily reach the resort town of Mammoth Lakes, the location of Lake District, it is difficult to imagine the hardships the miners endured to reach the mines. A thin ribbon of highway—Highway 395—hugs the base of the Sierra's eastern escarpment for most of its length, paralleling its snowy crest from Inyokern north to Bishop, Reno and Susanville. A three-hour drive south from Reno or a six-hour drive north from Los Angeles will take you to the sites of Lake District's old mining camps.

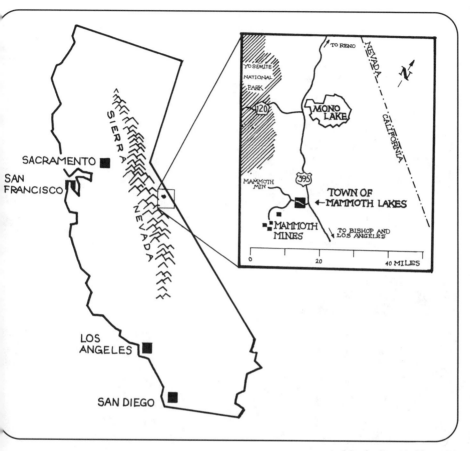

Map by Raymie Muzquiz

MAMMOTH GOLD
IN PERSPECTIVE

Although the shock waves generated by California's gold rush waned with each passing year, they were strong enough thirty years later that the barest rumor still sent men racing into the mountains to search every hillside and pan every stream. Thus it was that in 1875, lured by rumors of the elusive Lost Cement Mine, four prospectors discovered a promising quartz outcrop on the eastern slope of the Sierra Nevada twenty-four miles south of Mono Lake. Within two years a familiar pattern began to unfold—a pattern repeated countless times in the West's early mining history in such places as Red Dog Camp and Mad Mule Gulch and Chicken-Thief Flat—a pattern that would unfold once more amid the spectacular alpine setting of Lake Mining District. Here the boom and then the bust of Mammoth City would reflect, in microcosm, many of the characteristics common to California's frontier mining communities.

Like many camps, Mammoth City maintained a school, supported worthy causes, tolerated its prostitutes and discriminated against its Chinese residents. Like many, it was hurriedly built, on lots that daily increased in price—a restless camp, mirroring the inherent instability of the mining frontier. However, the lawlessness that often accompanied mining booms was notably absent in Mammoth City, despite its having "one well built jail." The newspapers vividly described the ceaseless flow of people and goods, coming and going. Especially the going. As Old Charley observed in 1888, "You know, folks shake the dust of a busted mining town like rats desert a sinking ship. They walk out an' leave everything, furniture and beds an' dishes on the table, maybe, like they et an' run" (Doyle 1935). It was said that the first to leave a town on the skids were the gamblers and prostitutes. Whether there was such a departure from Mammoth, contemporary accounts do not say. However, what they do say is that like many other mining towns, Mammoth City was ravaged by fire; unlike some, it did not recover.

Thirty Years after the Gold Rush

You may be surprised to find not a single picture of a bearded young man with a gold pan or a squinty-eyed prospector with a burro in this book. While these are the stereotypes often associated with gold mining, they don't hold true for Lake District, even though only thirty years had passed since the discovery of gold in the stream gravels of the western Sierra. The gold rush that began in 1849 was primarily a young man's adventure. Half of those who came were between the ages of twenty and thirty; many were in their teens. Many were from solid financial backgrounds, for traveling to California was expensive. Whether one came around the Horn, or via Panama by boat or overland by covered wagon, the trip was extremely difficult and dangerous. It was said that the timid never started and the weak died on the way. Once arrived at "the diggins," it was each man for himself, seeking his fortune there but intending to return home as soon as he filled his pockets with gold. Free from authority, cut loose from social restraints and the protection of law, and without wives and families, many of the gold seekers in the wilder camps indulged in drinking, gambling, fighting and shooting, as TV and the movies show us over and over.

Social upheaval was always close at hand, as soon as word spread about the next strike. Needing stability and social organization, many miners started miners' associations, anchors during a time of near-anarchy. But by 1879 much had changed. The transcontinental railroad had been completed; the trip to California, while still expensive, was no longer dangerous and lengthy. Lake District was a far cry from the crude, rough camps of the forty-niners who lived on beans, dried apples, flapjacks and salt pork. Many men brought their wives and children, and many were considerably over thirty. Mammoth City was generally law-abiding, with few shootings and killings. There was a feeling of community, with much support for the school. Few people talked of "going home." They had come west to stay, and if this camp folded, they would move on to another or start looking for a farm.

During the the thirty years following the gold rush, California changed mightily. In 1845 the total population was about 7,000, with but 680 Americans and the balance Spaniards and Mexicans. In the spring of 1849 there were just fifteen non-Hispanic women in San Francisco. By 1860, nine percent of the state's population were Chinese. By 1880, the total population was 865,000. Of those who were foreign-born, the majority came from the British Isles.

The stresses resulting from this influx of peoples who had never before rubbed shoulders with each other manifested themselves in some unpleasant ways. In many camps in 1849 and '50, the first French miners were driven forcibly from their claims. Many camps forbade Chinese from working or holding claims. Mexicans from Sonora, who were experienced miners and who even gave the Mother Lode its name *(Veta Madre)*, were not welcome either. In 1850 the state enacted a foreign miners' tax of twenty dollars a month, collected chiefly from Mexican miners. In 1851 the tax was reduced and then repealed, only to be reinstated in 1852 as a three-dollar and then four-dollar a month "license fee," levied mainly against Chinese and other "ineligible-for-citizenship" Asians. The overall result was that during the first years of the gold rush, the gold went to the Americans and Anglo-Europeans.

Analysis of Lake District's 1880 census reveals that, like most camps, the majority, although they hailed from many countries and many states, were English-speaking. Further analysis discloses some interesting findings. Only five of the eleven Confederate states were represented in this Reconstruction-era mining camp, and only three of those were from the Deep South. The seventeen Southerners made up only three percent of the population. This percentage, when compared to the number of Southerners working on Union Pacific Railroad crews or riding the Plains, is surprisingly small. Many former Confederate soldiers, unskilled and facing a shattered homeland, signed on to build the eastern portion of the transcontinental railroad. Others migrated west to Texas and became cowboys on the months-long trail drives. So why so few Southerners in Lake District? Too far away? Perhaps. Unlike the gold rush days, too little promise? Maybe. And maybe we'll never know. And maybe there's a theme for someone's research.

Southerners and Northerners, Americans and Europeans—in general, all got along with each other in the mines, and all looked down on other peoples. Toward the Indians, they reflected the government's policy, which did not grant United States citizenship and its rights to native Americans until 1924, after the government had finished taking their lands. In California's mining camps, Indians, Chinese, Mexicans and Blacks were more or less invisible and generally considered less than human. So it was in Lake District.

Hard-rock Mining

Most eastern Sierra discoveries, such as the Mammoth, differed in one all-important respect from the early finds on the Sierra's western slope. Prospectors on the eastern slope found few placers, those legendary deposits where anyone with a gold pan might find nuggets in a streambed. Instead, they found the gold and silver embedded in underground quartz veins. It is for good reason that mining such veins is called hard-rock mining. No electricity and no steam-engines powered the earliest mines and mills—only water power and the brute strength of men, mules and oxen. Let Mark Twain, who labored briefly as both miner and mill worker in Virginia City (one week in the latter capacity), strip the glamour from hard-rock mining:

> I had already learned how hard and long and dismal a task it is to burrow down into the bowels of the earth and get out the coveted

ore; and now I learned that the burrowing was only half of the work.... We had to turn out at six in the morning and keep at it till dark.... It is a pity that Adam could not have gone straight out of Eden into a quartz mill, in order to understand the full force of his doom to "earn his bread by the sweat of his brow." (Clemens 1872)

Like most hard-rock camps, Mammoth City was totally dependent on a single company for its economic health, its social well-being and, in fact, for its very existence. Few prospectors tried to work their own claims, for quartz mining required hundreds of feet of underground workings, expensive machinery, large mills and skilled men to operate them. The best the prospector could do was to sell his claim to a company that had enough capital and credit to pay its bills for months or even years before it produced a single ounce of gold. If the company failed, as did the Mammoth Mining Company, jobs vanished and the community quickly collapsed.

Imaginary Mines

Some aspects of mining have changed little. Mining is just as risky today as yesterday, with rumor and secrecy, exaggeration and optimism the norm. (Remember the uranium rush of the 1950s, when city folk became instant prospectors and, lugging geiger counters, swarmed over the hills of the western states, including Mammoth?) Con men ply their trade today just as they did a hundred years ago, dazzling the greedy and the gullible with stories of successful mines and luring them into highly speculative or fraudulent ventures. No one has described the hazards of mining investments better than Mark Twain, who lived amidst one of the great mining booms of all time at the Comstock Lode during the 1860s and '70s:

Every one of these wildcat mines—not mines, but holes in the ground over imaginary mines—was incorporated and had handsomely engraved "stock" and the stock was salable, too. It was bought and sold with a feverish avidity in the boards every day. You could go up on the mountainside, scratch around and find a ledge (there was no lack of them), put up a "notice" with a grandiloquent name in it, start a shaft, get your stock printed, and with nothing whatever to prove that your mine was worth a straw, you could put your stock on the market and sell out for hundreds and even thousands of dollars. To make money, and make it fast, was as easy as it was to eat your dinner.... There was NOTHING in the shape of a mining claim that was not salable. (Clemens 1872)

Those who made the fast bucks in the gold rush camps and in Virginia City in 1863 no doubt made them in Mammoth City as well. Profits went to those who "mined" the miners (grocers, hardware and dry goods merchants, prostitutes); to those who speculated in mining stocks and real estate and got out well before the bust; or perhaps to the superintendent who was rumored to have sacks of rich ore in his office—we'll come to him later on.

Revivals

Following the Mammoth Mining Company's failure and the town's collapse, Lake District experienced still another segment of the pattern—revivals based on sporadic, short-lived reopenings of old mines or based on new equipment and new methods that promised riches where others had failed. Arch Mahan's Mammoth Consolidated Mine, worked from 1927 to 1933, A. E. Beauregard's Monte Cristo Mine, worked during the 1940s and '50s, and the on-going operations of the Mammoth Lakes Mining Corporation are the most recent attempts to find profits in claims that were first surveyed in 1879. Most likely they will not be the last. According to some, the richest vein was never cut—but that is ahead of our story.

DISCOVERY

The gold rush came a bit later to the eastern Sierra. Eleven years later, to be exact. But when it did come, it was every bit as frenzied as the stampede to the western slope that followed James Marshall's 1848 gold discovery in the Sierra Nevada foothills. East of the Sierra Nevada, however, the rush became a gold-and-silver rush as miners there uncovered rich ledges of silver ore as well as gold. Prospectors washing gravel for placer gold below Mount Davidson started it all when in 1859 they discovered that the heavy blue-black gravel and sand they had been cursing and throwing away was incredibly rich silver ore.

Thousands who had just recently plodded west across the mountains frantically retraced their trails back over the Sierra, heading for the fabulous Comstock Lode east of Lake Tahoe. Rumors and dreams spurred some to range farther, east into the forbidding desert mountains and south along the Sierra to prospect its eastern slope. Word spread that Mormon miners had found "traces" at Dogtown, south of Bridgeport. Then news of gold near Mono Lake, in the large wash east of Conway Grade, brought seven hundred men racing to Monoville. New strikes followed each other before news of the last ones had cooled. Rich quartz veins northeast of Monoville spawned the wildly speculative camp of Aurora, which mushroomed into a town of 5,000 people and seventeen mills. Silver was discovered at Blind Springs Hill near Benton. Gold and silver at Bodie, north of Mono Lake.

Contributing to the frenzy was the excitement over some reddish, rusty-looking lava or *cement* (as it came to be called) "thickly spangled with flakes of purest gold" (Wright 1984). Whether this was a real find or total fantasy we may never know, but no matter. What is important to our story is that beginning in the 1860s the legendary Lost Cement Mine "somewhere on the headwaters of the Owens River" drew hundreds of prospectors to the eastern Sierra slope south of Mono Lake. Among them were B. S. Martin, B. N. Lowe, N. D. Smith and James A. Parker. On 20 June 1877, while prospecting about 800 feet up the western face of Mineral Hill, 24 miles south of Mono Lake, they discovered a promising ledge of ore-bearing quartz and staked out the Alpha claim. As the *Mammoth City Herald* of 27 December 1879 told the story, samples of the ore sent to Bodie assayed between $86 and $200 per ton. The original four—together with Al Jardine, John Briggs, Hank Rodgers, Harry Williams, W. R. Armstrong, J. C. Brown, L. M. Read, and A. J. Wren—began locating claims, "each location containing the full size, as allowed by the law of May 10th, 1872, 1500 by 600 feet." Parker, while filing the locations of the Alpha and Mammoth claims, gave the area its official name, Lake District.

These first claimants, following the usual procedure in new mining camps, elected Parker as District Recorder. (Parker, with P. A. Chalfant, had started Owens Valley's first newspaper, the *Inyo Independent,* in 1870.) This custom of choosing a recorder, to file and keep track of claims, served quite well to keep order under conditions that otherwise could have led to bloodshed and chaos. Surveys were not always accurate and, with men rushing to file claims, it was inevitable that some claim boundaries would overlap and that arguments would arise over who filed first.

Perhaps Mineral Hill (also called Gold Mountain and today known as Red Mountain) was really discovered two years earlier. John H. Ryan, in a report dated 1902, stated that Wren and Briggs —who had been grubstaked by their companions, Steward and Folk (or Foulk)—located the original Mammoth claims in 1875. But as W. A. Chalfant later observed, "If so, they did no more than post location notices. Discovery of the Alpha reminded them of their claim, and on July 30, 1877, Wren and Briggs located the Mammoth" (1947).

The Geologic Setting

Sweating, blasting, digging and hauling, prospectors rapidly covered the slopes of Mineral Hill with claims, pits and portals at elevations ranging from 8700 to 10,600 feet. They soon found that all of the gold and silver deposits were in a narrow zone, half a mile wide and two and a half miles long, of old volcanic rock called *latite*. This rock was formed about 190 million years ago (probably earliest Jurassic) when ancient volcanoes erupted enormous quantities of ash and lava over a vast area, forming layered volcanic deposits up to five miles thick. Later, mountain-building forces tilted and squeezed these volcanic layers and then a great mass of molten granitic rock intruded them. The once-molten granite forms much of today's Sierra Nevada; Mineral Hill with its ore-bearing veins is a remnant of the cooked, squeezed and deformed (metamorphosed) older volcanic rock.

The heat and pressure generated by the intrusion, over millions of years, altered the overlying volcanic rock significantly. Hot liquids and gases charged with various chemicals given off by the molten granite forced their way upward through cracks and pores in the ancient rock. Whenever conditions of temperature and pressure were just right, these liquids and gases deposited one mineral after another as veins within the overlying rock. The veins of Mineral Hill, mostly quartz and silicate minerals, commonly contain auriferous pyrite, free gold, pyrrhotite, arsenopyrite, sphalerite and chalcopyrite. The same process nearly saturated the overlying rock with pressurized mineralizing fluids and dispersed pyrite (iron sulfide, "fools' gold") in tiny crystals through much of it. The oxidized (rusted) pyrite colors the entire zone bright red-brown, hence the name Red Mountain.

Lake District prospectors also found that gold and silver did not occur uniformly throughout the quartz veins but appeared here and there, quite unpredictably. Reports on this and other aspects of the ore are consistent. According to Chalfant, the ore struck by the Mammoth's tunnels was in crystalline rocks, with gold occurring in pockets. Ryan's 1902 report notes that the vein was "semi-crystalline to a crystalline quartz" and "is from 40 to 60 feet in width." In fact, he says, "all quartz in this property is mineralized and carries gold, and more or less silver." According to the April 1904 *Mining and Scientific Press*, "the ores here also contain iron, lead, copper and zinc sulphides." H. A. Whiting, mining engineer, wrote a first-hand account of Mono County mines for the *Eighth Annual Report of the State Mineralogist*. Visiting Lake District in 1888, when most of the workings were still accessible, he described the ore-bearing veins as steeply dipping, a few feet to a few tens of feet thick:

> The veins of the Mammoth series strike northwesterly and dip eastwardly at 70 degrees to 80 degrees, conforming in this respect with the stratification planes of their inclosing rocks. The veinstone of their ore bodies is generally a hard, semi-crystalline to crystalline quartz.... Through this quartz the pay ore is distributed in bunches and spots, the veinstone being mineralized by magnetite and other oxides of iron and by auriferous pyrite, chalcopyrite, bornite, blende, and native gold. Although no characteristically developed silver minerals were observed, these ores are argentiferous.

Chapter 3 ✑

THE MAMMOTH
MINING COMPANY

The fickle mining world briefly turned its attention to newly-formed Lake District in the spring of 1878 when, in company with other San Francisco investors, Milton Lambeth, Edward Clarke and General George S. Dodge came to negotiate the purchase of the Mammoth claims. As bargaining proceeded, Dodge and his party examined assay reports and samples of ore. One sample, from a tunnel 400 feet below Mineral Hill's basaltic cap, reportedly tapped 100,000 tons of ore assaying $75 a ton in gold and silver. Remi Nadeau (1965) gives us this dramatized version of the occasion:

> One of the earliest to arrive was General George S. Dodge, a noted California mining investor. Owners of one of the mines showed him their property, offered ore samples and quoted assay figures. Dodge sat down on a pine stump...and looked up a thousand feet to the Mammoth outcroppings. "I don't want to know how rich they are," he answered. "They'll do for a deal anyhow."

There has been some confusion about the identity of General Dodge. Chalfant and others have stated that George S. Dodge "of Union Pacific fame" came to look at the Mammoth properties. However, it was a different General Dodge, *Grenville M. Dodge,* who was chief surveyor for the Union Pacific. According to Union Pacific records, he never set foot in Lake District and had no financial relationship with the Mammoth Mining Company. (The military titles stemmed from the recently concluded Civil War.) General George S. Dodge was a prominent California mining investor. His obituary—he died at age 42, within a year of organizing the Mammoth Mining Company—gives an overview of his business interests:

> [Dodge] was widely known in mining circles. He was a native of Vermont and served through the war of the Rebellion.... At the close of the war he was appointed Consular-General to one of the German cities, from whence he came to the Pacific Coast. His first mining operation of prominence was the purchase of a large interest in the Eureka Consolidated mine, which he successfully developed. He then bought into the Northern Belle mine; then into the General Thomas, Commanche, Mammoth and Headlight mines successfully. He...made an unsuccessful attempt to extract gold from the Oregon beach black sand. He was also a considerable loser in the celebrated diamond swindle. Some three years ago he was struck with paralysis, from which he never recovered. Towards the close of his life he suffered untold agonies. (Oakland *Daily Times,* 25 August 1881)

For the Mammoth group of five claims, Dodge and his associates paid $10,000 cash and $20,000 worth of stock in the company they organized immediately. It resembled the company Dodge had organized just seven months before to finance the McClinton Mine in Bodie. That company was incorporated on 3 November 1877 with 60,000 shares offered at $100 per share, for a total capitalization of $6,000,000. Dodge was president and treasurer, Edward Clarke superintendent. Dodge's new venture, the Mammoth Mining Company, was incorporated on 3 June 1878 with a capitalization of $10,000,000—100,000 shares of stock offered at $100 each. Dodge was president; Lambeth, Thomas Bell, and Solomon Heydenfeldt (also of the McClinton Mine) directors and trustees; and Clarke superintendent. Other directors mentioned in the initial organization were A. C. Rose, Jr., J. F. Haggin and George W. Grayson. Company headquarters were 302 Montgomery Street, San Francisco.

The Alpha, not a part of the Mammoth holdings, was bonded to speculators from Virginia City. The Armstrong Mine adjoining

Lake District's mining excitement focused on Mineral Hill. Most claims were located on its north and west slopes, pictured above. Twin Lakes below, center.

the Mammoth was also bonded, "for 120 days for $30,000, the bonder paying $2,500 cash for the privilege" *(Engineering and Mining Journal,* Vol. 27, 1879). Joseph Wasson noted these developments in the May 1878 *Mining and Scientific Press:*

> Lake District, 70 miles southwest [of Bodie], high in the Sierras, well wooded and watered, is attracting considerable attention and some work is doing. The ledges are very large and said to assay well. Gen. Geo. S. Dodge, largely interested in Bodie, is taking hold of Lake with his usual vigor.

On 5 June 1878 the San Francisco *Daily Stock Report* headlined, "A Mono County Bonanza...The Condition of the Company Justifies Brilliant Hopes." According to Ryan the company also obtained "water rights including dam, and in the neighborhood of 200 acres of timber land." Close at hand were water for power and a virgin forest that could be converted into fuel, lumber and shingles for a town and into timbers for building a mill and shoring the tunnels. News of Lake District's potential spread like wildfire and in no time

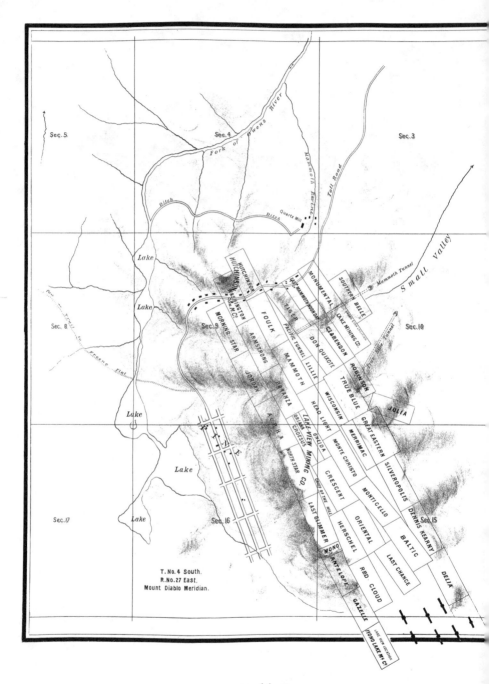

Sec. 5

Sec. 4

Fork of Owens River

Sec. 3

Kammoth Hartone

Toll Road

Ditch

Ditch

Quartz Mill

Lake

Small Valley

Lake

Mammoth Tunnel

HUTCHINSON

HUTCHINSON

WASHINGTON

No. 2 & M. Co.

MONUMENTAL

SOUTHERN BELLE

EAST MAMMOTH

LAKE MINING CO.

LILIE

CLARENDON

Sec. 8

Sec. 9

MORNING STAR

FOULK

ARMSTRONG

PACIFIC TUNNEL

DON QUIXOTE

ROBINSON

Sec. 10

Pass

MAMMOTH

JORDAN

BONANZA

LILIE

WISCONSIN

TRUE BLUE

GREAT EASTERN

JULIA

Lake

ALPHA

LAKE VIEW MINING CO.

HEAD LIGHT

OROMELLA

ONEIDA

CROESUS

MONTE CHRISTO

MERRIMAC

SILVEROPOLIS

Lake

NORTH STAR

ONE OF THE

CRESCENT

MONTICELLO

DENNIS KEARNY

Sec. 15

Sec. 17

Lake

Sec. 16

LAST GLIMMER

HILL

HERSCHEL

ORIENTAL

BALTIC

T. No. 4 South.
R. No. 27 East.
Mount Diablo Meridian.

MONO

ANTELOPE

RED CLOUD

LAST CHANCE

DELIA

GAZELLE

MONO LAKE M. CO.

LAKE VIEW LOCATION

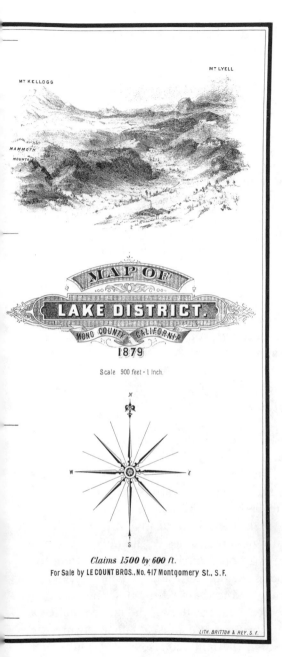

MT. LYELL

MT. KELLOGG

MAMMOTH
MOUNTA...

MAP OF LAKE DISTRICT.

MONO COUNTY CALIFORNIA

1879

Scale 900 feet - 1 Inch.

N

W   E

S

Claims 1500 by 600 ft.
For Sale by LE COUNT BROS., No. 417 Montgomery St., S.F.

This map shows the location of claims mentioned in the text. Note also: the trail to Fresno Flat, center left; the ditch (flume), center; Fork of Owens River (Mammoth Creek), center top; the toll road to Lake District, upper right. The small black rectangles on both sides of the road, center, indicate Mammoth City.

Pine City, shown by the grid on the east shore of the largest lake, Lake Mary, never materialized in this location. The Mammoth tunnel, shown driven in from the east, also never materialized. The decorative mountain scene in the upper right-hand corner (customary in nineteenth century maps) bears no relation to Lake District topography. The claim boundaries are probably accurate, but some portions of the map are not. For example, many of the tributaries to the lakes and the Owens River are fabrications.

Map courtesy of Henry E. Huntington Library

at all nineteen companies had stakes in the camp. Like many other discoveries of the time, the Mammoth group was dutifully hailed as "the largest bonanza outside Virginia City" and by the end of June of 1878, Mammoth City had an estimated population of 125.

The Mill and Flume

The Dodge group began construction that July of a twenty-stamp mill, although ore in quantity had not yet been produced or confirmed. But mining madness rarely leads to prudent decisions. Milton Lambeth stayed in the area to select a site and to arrange for the mill's construction within ninety days. (Chalfant mentions Milton *Sambeth,* but original papers reflected in the *Pacific Coast Annual Mining Review* list him as *Lambeth.)* He chose a mill site half a mile below the mines.

Erected on a quarter-acre, the milling complex reportedly cost $160,000 and required 800,000 feet of lumber. The main support timbers were a foot square "to withstand the heavy snows of the region" (Chalfant 1947). Machinery for the mill was hauled in from the south by freight wagon. The mill contained twenty stamps, each weighing 900 pounds. Each stamp dropped onto a mortar, crushing the ore that moved continuously into it. Mortar and stamp together were called a battery. Driven by a six-foot Knight water wheel (which in turn drove a 20-foot flywheel) under a 175-foot head of water, the stamps could effectively maintain a cycle of 100 drops of six to eight inches per minute. The Knight wheel was selected because it was designed for water of high pressure but low volume. The Twin Lakes flume delivered just such water.

That a flume had to be built at all tells us something about where water was *not* in 1878. Despite the many lakes in the area, no water flowed naturally near the mines or the mill. The flume was initially constructed as an open ditch, carrying water from the outlet of Twin Lakes around the northern slope of Panorama Dome to the mill. But after snow and ice blocked the flow the very first winter, the flume was roofed. Construction of the flume required a tremendous expenditure of time and muscle, all to ensure the uninterrupted flow of water, the mill's sole source of power. Nor

Frasher Collection, Pomona Public Library. Print courtesy USFS, Inyo National Forest.

The Mammoth Mining Company stamp mill about 1920. It has since vanished, but its 20-foot flywheel remains exactly where it was bolted together and set in place more than a hundred years ago. Monumental Rock (Mammoth Rock) and Mineral Hill on the skyline.

was there water near where the miners wanted to live, that is, until diversion works were built on the east shore of Lake Mary to bring water through Pine City to Mammoth City.

These water projects were costly and difficult undertakings. Nevertheless, prospects for the company seemed bright, if we are to judge by current news articles, such as this one in the October 1878 *Pacific Coast Annual Mining Review* (note, however, that the tunnel has not yet cut the lode):

The company is vigorously at work developing their property, having already put up a first-class 20-stamp mill, driven by water-power, to which the ore is carried from the mine by chute and tramway. In view of the large quantity of ore the mine is likely to yield, it is proposed to increase the number of stamps as soon as possible. This lode, which carries a rich gold and silver-bearing ore, is from 60 to 70 feet in thickness, and crops out in great strength. The ore resembles that from the Comstock Lode, and assays at the rate of about $75 per ton. The ore in sight is estimated at about eighty thousand tons. The tunnel being driven will cut the lode at a depth of one thousand feet below the croppings, and will afford an adit for drainage and ore extraction to that depth. The company's mill has just started up, and bullion shipments are expected to be kept up continuously in the future.

Alas, bullion shipments were far from continuous. Despite the foot-square timbers, snow caved in one section of the mill during the first winter. The following summer the mill shut down for $80,000 worth of reinforcing and alteration, which doubled its capacity by adding twenty more stamps and an 80-horsepower steam engine. The steam engine was to serve as a backup power source for the mill, to maintain production if snow blocked the flume again. Although the 13 September 1879 *Mammoth City Herald* reported that the steam engine had been tested on at least one occasion, there is no evidence that it was ever used.

But such was the enthusiasm that a correspondent for the San Francisco *Daily Alta California* predicted that "within 30 or 40 days we shall see that this mine carries an appropriate name—Mammoth!" (5 June 1879). "Every idle man wanting work has it furnished by the Mammoth Company," trumpeted the *Herald* (30 July 1879). Under the watchful eye of Superintendent William Hardy, who had replaced Clarke, the rebuilt mill started up in October 1879. Maximum production was projected at 100 tons per twenty-four hours. The *Engineering and Mining Journal* of 15 November 1879 stated that during its first thirty days, the mill produced bullion worth $23,000. The *Mammoth City Times* for 12 July 1880 happily reported that output from the Mammoth's tunnels reached 75 tons a day, and the *Herald* for 31 July 1880 corroborated these production figures when it mentioned that the "Mammoth Company worked 525 tons of ore during the past week" in its forty-stamp mill.

This six-foot Knight wheel, under an effective head of about 175 feet, drove all of the stamp mill's machinery. The Knight wheel was a special type of water wheel, designed to maximize power from water of high pressure but low volume.

This flume from Twin Lakes delivered the water that powered the stamp mill. After snow choked the flume during the very first winter, the company covered it. Very little of the covering lumber remains; we can only guess that it was picked up for firewood. (1978 photo)

Three dumps, one below the other on the north slope of Mineral Hill (Red Mountain), mark the portals to the main workings of the Mammoth Mine. Though becoming fainter each year, they are still clearly recognizable. The fourth dump, at the lowest working, is hidden by the trees. Mammoth City was in the ravine at the base of the slope.

The Mammoth's Four Tunnels

The Mammoth Mine, by far the largest operation in Lake District, consisted of the five claims recorded as the Foulk, Armstrong, San Francisco, Big Bonanza and Mammoth. The company developed its claims through four tunnels, one above the other. Each adit, driven in a southeasterly direction into the northern slope of Mineral Hill, was more than 1200 feet. (A *tunnel,* strictly speaking, is a horizontal excavation going *through* a mountain. As I use it here, however, it means the horizontal passageway leading from the surface into the mountain. Mammoth City newspapers used the term in this more general sense and so did the miners. A*dit* is the proper mining term for the horizontal passage leading into a mine. The *portal* is the

This mine portal (c. 1860), although not in Lake District, illustrates construction with hand-hewn timbers. Since isolated mines were seldom near lumber mills and hardware stores, miners had to manage with whatever was at hand. Even though part of the walls and the roof have collapsed, this is a fine example of square-cut timbering. Note the reinforcing along the sides and the top.

entrance to a mine. These and other mining terms are defined in a special section after chapter fifteen titled "Mining Terms.")

Reported elevations of the portals have varied through the years, as surveying techniques became more precise. In 1977 the Mammoth Lakes Mining Corporation had its property surveyed by aerial photography, which showed the altitude of its dump on the northwest slope to be exactly 9,000 feet. Based on its maps, the elevations for the old portals are, from top to bottom, 9,210 feet, 9,130 feet, 8,875 feet and 8,770 feet. The present road's elevation is 8,694 or 76 feet below the portal of tunnel four. During the mining era, Mammoth Avenue (south of the present road) was just about level with the portal.

Tunnel one, on the steep slope below Mineral Hill's basaltic cap, 200 feet below the summit, was the highest of the four. It went in over 1500 feet, with its first cross-cut on the south side, forty-five feet in from the portal. It produced little ore and no assay reports exist. People have wondered whether the miners working the higher levels lived in the mine in summer, or whether they lived in cabins above, on the broad, flattish crest of Mineral Hill. (Storms and snow precluded working them most of the winter. We do know that miners worked the Mammoth's lower tunnels throughout the winter and that, in the Headlight and Monte Cristo joint tunnel, crews cut 560 feet between 1 December 1879 and 24 March 1880.) Although contemporary sources do not comment on the higher tunnels, when printed accounts are absent, archaeological detective work has enabled us to fill some of the gaps.

My own investigations indicate that living *in,* rather than living *above* the mine, was the custom of the day. Several factors argue against the proposition that the six- to eight-man crews lived on the crest above, walking down 300 feet to the portals in the morning and back up the talus slope in the evening. First, the nearest cabin foundations are not close to the portals but are about a third of a mile to the south, just below the crest of Mineral Hill, in the trees. These foundations always occur close to exploratory pits, suggesting that they belonged to prospectors who were working their own claims. Second, a trip both down and up a steep talus slope has its hazards, doubly dangerous in the dark of night. The clincher for me, however, was my findings in tunnel one, prior to the 1980 earthquakes that buried the portal under tons of talus. I found shelves chiseled into the rock along both sides of the entrance. Farther in I found more shelves, which still held a candle holder, ax head, ink bottle, and medicine bottles and small tin cans containing catarrh remedies, cough medicine, herbine (a vegetable tonic), salves, pills, and talcum powder. In addition, in the "living quarters" of tunnel one, I found evidence of a fire and large quantities of burnt, fuzed household glass. One additional argument: the talus above the upper levels is unstable and very dangerous. I was very nearly killed while climbing this slope in 1986, during research for this book. Forty square yards of talus suddenly started moving downhill, with myself unwillingly on board. Rock slides such as this and avalanches have completely covered the old portal.

Tunnel two, less than a hundred feet below tunnel one, reportedly produced the richest ore of all Lake District mines. The adit was 1500 feet and cut the vein 800 feet in. Although we have no reliable assays from the 1870s, in 1902 Ryan reported on samples taken from tunnels two and three. Three samples were taken from random locations outside tunnel two's partially caved in portal. One taken in front of the portal assayed $8.38 per ton, $4.13 gold and $4.25 silver. One taken from a slide west of the portal assayed $14.34 per ton, $10.74 in gold and $3.60 in silver. The third, taken from the dump, assayed $7.93 per ton, $4.13 in gold and $3.80 in silver.

Two hundred and fifty feet farther down the slope, tunnel three's 1,250-foot adit cut the vein 600 feet in. The first crosscut, 490 feet in, was driven fifty feet. Samples taken 431 feet into the adit showed a trace of silver and gold valued at $3.30 per ton. Tunnel four, the lowest, was 1,650 feet. The first crosscut, 465 feet in, extended 87 feet and was reported to be entirely in quartz. The second crosscut, 1,105 feet in, extended 50 feet.

The Mammoth and Nearby Mines

The first survey of the Mammoth Mining Company's property was made on 5 and 6 June 1878. General Dodge himself signed the requests and paid for the surveys of the Mammoth and Headlight mines. In a formal sworn statement, U.S. Deputy Mineral Surveyor William Minto wrote that the "present owners have commenced, and are diligently prosecuting, work on a tunnel" and that "a twenty stamp quartz mill has been contracted for and is in course of construction. Total expenses already incurred cannot be less than $10,000" (U.S. General Land Office). He then notes the company's interest in an adjacent mine, the Head Light (or Headlight). "The tunnel and mill are, however, designed for the working of the Head Light Mine, joining Mammoth on the south, in common with the latter, a two-thirds interest in the Head Light being held by the owners of the Mammoth." In his survey of the Head Light the next day, Minto comments, "The quartz contains Gold and Silver of about equal value and presents the same general appearance as in the Mammoth of which it is a continuation." (In the 1980s the quartz being mined from the old Headlight and adjacent mines contained 20 to 40 parts of silver to one part gold, which gave silver values significantly lower than gold values.)

The Monte Cristo (or Christo) Mine, when it was located on 16 April 1878, was considered to be "the southern extension of the HeadLight Mine." U.S. Deputy Mineral Surveyor W. S. Lilien, who surveyed it on 9 July 1879, reported that the Monte Christo Mining Company had spent on labor and improvements "not less than one thousand dollars. Said improvements consist of shafts and drifts" (U.S. General Land Office).

The Mammoth, Headlight and Monte Cristo mines, believed to be on the same vein, were owned and worked by San Francisco mining companies. The Headlight and Monte Cristo, originally separate operations, were combined when the Monte Cristo Consolidated Mines Corporation incorporated in mid-1879 with six claims and a capitalization of $1,000,000. Presumably the Mammoth Mining Company maintained a major interest in this consolidation. Its major development was a joint tunnel near the Mammoth with a 1500-foot westerly-driven crosscut. Low-grade quartz was reported 1200 feet into the adit.

The Lisbon Mine, the only important mine in the district that was privately owned, operated profitably for a number of years. It held eight claims at the southern end of Mineral Hill's western slope. Its three adits, at an altitude of about 9500 feet and a hundred feet apart vertically, were driven in to cut a vein said to be two to six feet wide. According to Whiting, "The Lisbon lode is reported to be about two feet in width, and the ore a free milling gold quartz, with more or less auriferous pyrite, and without much occurrence of the more complex metallic sulphides common to the Mammoth series of veins" (1888). Although no figures are available, reports indicate that the Lisbon had good management and, operating more modestly than the Mammoth, worked low grade ore at a profit. Its five-stamp steam-powered mill constructed in 1885 ran steadily for several years.

Countless lesser claims clothed the slopes and the broad summit of Mineral Hill, each with its own exploratory pits and some with underground workings. The 1879 map of Lake District on pages 14–15, though fraught with geographical inaccuracies, shows forty-seven claims all properly located and filed. No doubt some were worked and may have produced ore. Unfortunately, however, production records—if they ever existed—have never been found; an occasional reference to one of the claims shows up now and then in Bodie or Bridgeport newspaper articles. Taking due note of Lake District's activity, a correspondent for the San Francisco *Daily Alta California* wrote:

> The mines are all looking very well. Here...all is activity, and the different developments are being pushed with vigor. Different companies are opening up their properties prior to shipping in mills. Some have some very fine showings, as the Don Quixote, True Blue, Silveropolis, Monte Cristo, Crescent, North Star, Alpha, Jordan, Armstrong, and many others, not to speak of of the Mammoth itself, the development of whose 40-foot ledge attracted so much attention to this camp. (24 July 1879)

Mammoth Company Stock

New mines were front-page news in the 1860s and '70s, particularly in San Francisco, the financial center of the West. Investors and speculators played the market in mining stocks perhaps even more wildly than they play the penny-stock market today. "At one time," according to Ryan, "the Mammoth Company's stock rose from 19 cents to $10 in ten days." In April 1879 miners struck ore "which was said to be 'half gold,' and excitement raged still higher" (Nadeau 1965). That July the stock rose to $15 a share. Franklin Buck, a Mammoth City businessman, thought the stock was worth a hundred dollars a share but at the same time, in a letter dated 29 June 1879, he cautioned his family in Maine against mining stocks.

> I see you are getting interested in stocks. Beware! For it's a terrible fascinating game. The whole people of the State of Nevada and California almost are playing at this game.... I believe the Mammoth Mine here to be the best buy in the lot. This mine is not run to put the stock up but for some game is kept back. They don't try

to take out bullion and grand show but sack up all the rich ore and work the front ore and work the poorest. Mr. [George W.] Grayson, the new President, is on his way here and I know him and will try and find out something, but this we all know: the ledge is immense and rich. They are running a tunnel at the base of the mountain and if they find the same ledge of gold ore as in the upper tunnel there is no telling the value of this mine. This will show a ledge 20 feet wide, 800 feet deep and of unknown length. The stock ought to be worth over 100 dollars a share. It is now selling for thirteen. You are too far off to deal in stocks.

By late October, 1879, Mammoth stock was down to $6.50, even though a Mammoth newspaper that month reported, "M. J. Parks, night foreman, brought in about twenty pounds of ore, gold mixed with quartz. Besides that lot, huge chunks were found, 10, 15, or 20 pounds, and one 50 pounds, alive with gold. The ore will assay $50,000 to $120,000 a ton" (Chalfant 1947). At the same time, Chalfant warns us to be skeptical of such assays. "The experienced reader need not be reminded of the prospector's tendency to feature the richest-looking piece of ore, though it be no larger than half a golf ball in size." But in Lake District, mining fever pushed aside all cautions. The 30 July 1879 *Herald* had reported, "No idle men in town. In consequence Mammoth City looks deserted in the day time." Both the *Bodie Standard* and the *Engineering and Mining Journal* forecast 100 stamps for the Mammoth mill.

The Tramway

Of all the Mammoth Company's projects, it was the tramway that was the most frustrating and made the company look ridiculously incompetent. While the mill was well constructed, the tramway perhaps best demonstrated the company's mismanagement. The first attempts to run loaded ore cars nearly killed two brakemen. Rebuilt several times, it never functioned effectively until mule power was reinstated. A strong, reliable mule proved to be more effective than any other method of controlling the ore cars, even though he lay down every time a stiff wind funneled through the canyon. The story goes that on one occasion a strong gust actually blew the mule off the track; ever after, that wise mule lay down

This cut was blasted through the rock for a section of the tramway, which carried ore from the mines to the mill. Other sections were built on stilts.

whenever he sensed a high wind, holding up production accordingly.

The tramway's difficulties centered on the various proposals for moving ore down 3500 feet of track from the tunnels high on Mineral Hill to the 500-ton ore bins at the mill. Since all the portals were on a near-vertical talus slope and tunnel two, the source of the richest ore, was high on the unstable face, the difficulties were real. After arranging for the mill's construction, the company speedily erected a bull wheel and tramway east of the tunnels on "rather shaky stilts" perhaps as early as 1878. But the winds that blew in part of the mill's roof also blew down part of the tram trestle. After considerable discussion, the company decided to build a covered tramway to protect the track as much as possible from wind and snow. One section would cut through rock and be roofed over with timbers; the other sections would have snow sheds built over the track. But seemingly no one thought of ice. On 12 November 1879 the *Times* lavished praise on the project and on Superintendent Hardy:

> The new covered tramway between the Mammoth mine and the mill went into operation this afternoon and proved a complete success. The tramway presents some curious features and is well worth a moment's observation. The cars which are of iron, hold about four tons each. They are run from the mine in trains of four each, by gravity, being controlled entirely by brakes of peculiar power. There are a great many sharp curves in the track, but the little trains go about them with perfect ease and safety. Arriving at the mill the cars are emptied and are then drawn back to the mine by a pair of mules. The tramway and cars were both built from designs by Superintendent Hardy.

A week later the *Times* printed an article notable for what it did *not* say. Although it expressed a growing doubt that the new tram would perform as well as the company predicted, it barely mentioned an accident that caused considerable damage as well as a near-fatality.

> The new tramway has been a source of considerable annoyance, during the week, to the Mammoth mill managers. One or two accidents have happened and the failure to get ore down caused a stoppage of the mill. The cars, which were built in Virginia City, are not what was expected by Col. Hardy, and a good many alterations have been made. The latest is a new and more powerful brake, and last night when the cars were sent down for the first time with this improvement, they worked satisfactorily. To-day the cars are making regular trips, and at noon the mill was started up, to Mr. Collier's [the mill manager] infinite delight.

But problems became apparent almost at once. As the *Times* pointed out just three weeks later, the track was laid with little technical know-how. On the curves, the outside rail was laid level with the inner one and "on one of the curves there [was] an actual depression of the outer rail." The snow sheds also had flaws. Because the cars could barely pass between the supporting timbers, anyone caught in the sheds when a load started down was consigned to a sure death. The *Times* reported with evident concern,

"For the same reason the brakeman could not jump off without crawling over the top of the cars, and even then there was barely room beneath the timbers." The design of the cars only added to the certainty of the grim fate that awaited the brakeman. He had to stand between the cars in order to operate the brake and "once underway, the [brakeman] was in about as complete a death trap as it is possible to invent." (The *Herald* stayed clear of this issue, perhaps for reasons we will discuss later.) On 6 December 1879, in a lengthy, scathing essay titled "A Great Railroad," the *Times* revealed all the mistakes the company had endeavored to keep quiet, heaping scorn upon the company's managers but sympathizing with the poor brakemen (both named Wright) and with the mule that would have to toil all the harder.

For a company composed of intelligent men, and controlled by gentlemen of experience in mining, we do think the Mammoth Mining Company has been the victim of more costly and ridiculous experiments than any mining enterprise we ever heard of. The latest failure in the line of operations is the new tramway, which as everybody knows was begun last summer, only finished a few weeks ago, and has cost a great deal of money—some say $14,000. After all this expenditure of time and money, the tramway is now pronounced a failure and is abandoned; the rails are torn up and about to be relaid on the old affair on stilts. This is not an unexpected result. While the thing was being dug out last summer, every one who knew anything about the science of railway building predicted that it wouldn't work. In the first place it was an absurdity to suppose that two loaded cars weighing five tons each, could be run by gravity and controlled on a grade of 580 feet to the mile, and around the sharp curves with which the line of survey abounded. The result abundantly proves that these predictions were correct. The very first attempt to run loaded cars down and control them by the brakes, nearly resulted in the death of Edward Wright.... It [the ore train] left the track at the first curve, smashed through the shedding, and tore things to pieces generally. Then the smart Alexanders who built the thing decided, that the cars must be provided with new and improved brakes. These were put on—brakes to press the rail, like those in use on the California street railroad in San Francisco. These worked well enough for a day or two—that is to say by excercising the greatest care, they could manage now and then, without any more serious misfortune than leaving the track a few times, to get to the mill in safety. Finally, the other day the rain and storm brought matters to a crisis. The snow and rain blew into the openings under the roof left to furnish light, formed ice on the track, and—well it was the old story. Charles Wright started down the steep grade with two cars, his back actioned brake that was warranted not to cut in the eye or run down at the heel, slipped over the rail like a piece of bacon rind.... When he saw that it was no use, he tried to jump from the flying cars, but before he could do so, the latter struck one of the fatal curves, jumped the track, and went crashing through the timbers of the shedding, ore, cars, timbers, brakes and poor Wright, all lying in an undistinguishable mass.... That accident sealed the fate of the tramway. Nobody could be got to run the cars, the mill was standing idle for want of ore, and Mr. Hardy promptly decided to put the old thing on stilts, which by the way had been partially torn down.... In a week or two...the mule and his train of little dumps will be in full operation.

On 14 January 1880 *Evening Express* correspondent George Forbes commented on these difficulties to his Los Angeles readers:

A covered tramway, half a mile in length, was built from the mine to the mill. The Superintendent, the foreman of the mine, both declared the grade too heavy and the curves too short, but, on the plans being submitted to San Francisco, they were ordered to proceed. No breaks [sic] could control the loaded cars; they ran with apparent ease and frightful velocity when the wheels were deadlocked; jumped the curves like a frisky boy going over a snowbank; nearly killed a man or two; ran nearly through the mill, missing several men by almost a miracle, when they were unfortunately induced to pass the said curves; and conducted themselves so outrageously that no man could be found to take them in charge. The tramway was abandoned and is being taken up at intervals.

Forbes's assertion, that both the superintendent and foreman said the grade was too steep and the curves too short but were ordered to proceed anyway, is particularly interesting. For it contradicts the *Times* report above that the tramway and cars were designed by Hardy. Could Forbes's article, written a month after the tramway's failure, have been Hardy's attempt to distance himself from responsibility for the fiasco?

Edward Wright, the unfortunate brakeman of the first Mammoth Mine Special, received special mention. Along with some sarcastic comments about the tramway, the 19 November *Times* noted Wright's new employment:

> Ed Wright, the young man who the other day tried to demonstrate that a four ton car, with a pop gun brake, could be safely run down a railroad on a grade of nearly 500 feet to the mile, and made a most wretched failure of it, has retired from the Mammoth employ and gone to canvassing for a book. The latter he says is a hazardous employment, but after his experience on the new tramway he wouldn't be afraid to walk up to a cannon's mouth.

A Fraud? A Scam?

Already we can see glimmerings of what may have caused the company's failure. By October 1879 the mill had been enlarged to forty stamps, giving it a capacity of 100 tons of ore every twenty-four hours. Its ore bins would hold 500 tons. The little four-car trains coming down the face of Mineral Hill could carry sixteen tons maximum; most of the time they carried considerably less. After many trips to fill those ore bins, the trains would then need to make eight to ten trips every single day to keep the bins full and the mill operating. But by December 1879, a year and a half after General Dodge and friends had started construction, the mill still lacked a reliable supply of ore. The company had spent thousands of dollars building a mill, buying stamps and a steam engine, digging a flume, and driving four adits deep into Mineral Hill. Yet building the tramway, a crucial link in the operation, was a bumbling, haphazard effort that never did solve the problem of keeping a steady stream of ore flowing to the mill day after day. Clearly something is out of focus here. Neither the *Herald* nor the *Times* nor anyone else raised the question of why the mill was not built close to the mines in the first place.

There is reason to wonder whether the Mammoth Mining Company from the very beginning was a fraud. Could it have been a stock scam? Or could management have deliberately skimmed off the high grade ore? Franklin Buck thought not, believing (in his letter quoted previously) the company a better investment than the Bodie mines. "This mine is not run to put the stock up but for some game is kept back. They don't try to take out bullion and grand show...."

Chapter 4

LAKE DISTRICT'S CAMPS

As winter snows melted in the spring of 1879 and news of the Mammoth Mine spread north, south, and west across the Sierra, more gold seekers poured into Lake District. Among them was Franklin Buck of Maine, mentioned in the preceding chapter. He had arrived in San Francisco in August of 1849, after a long voyage of 195 days. He was then twenty-three years old—five feet eleven inches tall, 175 pounds, well proportioned, with dark red hair and beard. He read the classics (Homer's *Iliad* was his favorite), knew French, and learned Spanish on the voyage to California. The book, *A Yankee Trader in the Gold Rush,* contains letters he wrote between 1846 and 1881. His letters from Bodie and Mammoth City are a very personal account of life in Lake District and an invaluable source of first-hand information. A sure case of gold fever permeates this letter he wrote from Bodie to his family in Maine. He is now fifty-two years old.

> Just after my arrival a rich strike was made in the Mammoth Mine at Lake District, 50 miles south. Some of the specimens were half gold. I hitched up the horses...and got there in three days. This mine is on top of the Sierra Nevadas...and the snow is still three feet deep. It's a beautiful place. Grand peaks rise all around and there are seven lakes right above the town and lots of pine timber and water. Three miles below the valley is green with the new grass.

I like the country about here. It is the best mineral country that I know of. Rich mines all around and I shall spend the summer trying get hold of one. It's the only way to make money. I have several chances to go in now. If you are lucky you make a fortune. (16 April 1879)

Two weeks later he was writing, "I received a letter from you which Jennie sent. Hereafter direct to Mammoth City, Mono County, Cal., as I go over there tomorrow to stay." And stay he did, for well over a year.

Mineral Park

Besides Mammoth City, three other mining camps had already mushroomed within Lake District: Mineral Park, Mill City and Pine City, half a mile apart. At the foot of the grade, west of the meadow and condominiums, along today's Old Mammoth Road lay Mineral Park. So named, wrote George W. Forbes (with tongue in cheek?), "because no trace of mineral has ever been found in the vicinity"

The old sawmill east of Lake District, whose ruins are pictured above and opposite, may have been built as early as the 1860s. Its timbers very likely resemble
those of the Mineral Park and Sherwin Creek sawmills. These photos show how
a strong, solid structure was built without a single bolt or nail. Joints are carefully fitted, and wooden pegs and wedges hold the timbers together. (1988 photo)

(22 Jan. 1880). Forbes, as noted previously, was a correspondent for
the Los Angeles *Evening Express;* his observations of Lake District,
like Buck's, are among the best that we have. At Mineral Park he
noted "a saw mill, brewery, stores and saloons scattered among the
pines." The 1880 census listed also a hotel, stable and pasture,
boarding house, toll house and a dozen cabins. The sawmill Forbes
mentioned, owned by John McFarland and Robert Fraser, was the
sole reason for Mineral Park's existence. The sawmill itself was
located above Mineral Park, "a few hundred yards below" the Mammoth mill complex, according to the *Mammoth City Herald.* After
running the sawmill two and a half years, McFarland wanted out of
the partnership. His father, sixty-eight-year-old Samuel McFarland,
replaced him and continued with Fraser to operate the steam-powered mill and sell its lumber throughout the district.

The *Herald's* account of Mineral Park's development said that by the spring of 1878 George Rowan

> was moving in a heavy stock of general merchandise—the first to arrive in this section. He established himself at the foot of the grade, about a mile below the mill, at what is now called Mineral Park. There were no accomodations then save a few scattering brush houses and canvass tents in that portion of the district. Rowan's store was a large tent. The large hewn log house now used by Rice and Hause as a hotel, was rapidly pushed to completion and opened as an eating house and saloon by Ashley, Morris and Kirk Stevens. Robt. Frazer and others came in near this time to look out a site for a sawmill, which he soon after brought in and erected a few hundred yards below where the Mammoth mill now stands. There was no house of any importance, but a stockade was being built by Vince Higgins for a blacksmith shop. (7 April 1880)

Half a mile up the road from Mineral Park Forbes found Mill City, the site of company headquarters and the mill. In the census of 1880, Mill City was lumped together with Mammoth City.

> Up a still steeper grade and we are in Mill City, the headquarters of the Mammoth Company and where their mill is situated. Inspection among the pines and firs failed to find any trace of the 'city'. To be sure, there is a store, several cabins, a rickety hay and feed yard, a slaughter pen and the walls of some building in course of erection.... (22 Jan. 1880)

Mammoth City

Another half-mile up the road lay Mammoth City, the center of the district and by far the largest of the four camps. But before commenting on the town, Forbes mentioned a characteristic of the region that visitors today commonly experience:

> The first thing which strikes the stranger in Mammoth is the exceeding lightness of the air. As he wends his way up the steep gradients known as streets he puffs, gasps and actually stops for lack of breath till he becomes somewhat accustomed to the rarified atmosphere.

Once he caught his breath, Forbes said that Mammoth City

> can be called the city of two streets, one running parallel to the cañon, the other diverging from it at an acute angle as we ascend.

We can see by stakes and cabins planted here and there among the rocks and stumps in the ravines and along the hillside that prospective Mammoth occupies a large area. As it stands at present, two streets, approximately half a mile in length, flanked by the most temporary of temporary buildings—with a few exceptions—constitute the somewhat famous city. (22 Jan. 1880)

Actually, the newspapers referred to several streets, suggesting that Mammoth City may have had four streets: Main Street (also called Mammoth Avenue), which was sixty feet wide according to the 15 November 1880 *Herald;* Washington Street, which ran parallel to Main Street; a toll road above and below Main Street; and Central Avenue. The latter probably ran at right angles to Main and Washington streets, connecting them and perhaps continuing down the slope to connect with tunnel four, providing a route for supplies and equipment.

The shelters that Forbes described as "the most temporary of temporary buildings" probably were canvas tents or brush lean-tos, which newcomers to mining camps often lived in while more substantial dwellings were hurried to completion. However, he neglects to mention that the miners who stayed year-round needed sturdy cabins in order to survive the formidable winters. They often dug their foundations into the hillsides, lined them with rocks for strength and warmth, built the sides of rocks and logs and laid stout roofs on top. Although now overgrown with brush, many of Mammoth City's rock-lined foundations are still recognizable.

Buck's letters from Bodie, 16 and 30 April 1879, give us more details of Mammoth City and exude confidence in its future:

There is a small town of 15 or 20 houses, a large mill run by water power and every facility for mining cheap. I liked the place so much that I bought a lot and shall probably spend the summer there. There are a dozen other mines in the vicinity and I anticipate a grand rush to the new place. In two weeks there will be plenty of lumber cheap and I shall put up two buildings.

I have been waiting for lumber to build. Shall put up a building 20 x 40, two stories. Have a half a dozen applications for it now. Can build it for about $800 and rent it for 150 dollars a month. My lot, 25 x 112 feet, cost 125 dollars. Could sell it now for $250. The mining experts and capitalists who have visited the lake district speak highly of the mines. Have bought several. Will open them out and put up mills and we expects a grand rush. It will be a lovely place in the summer but too much snow to do much in the winter. I expect to make money enough this summer to go away in the winter, if I am in luck. But I think it will last for several years.

Mines and miners needed food, drink, shelter, lumber, horses, stables, clothing, machinery, tools and hundreds of other items. Suppliers eager to fill these needs followed the rushes to new camps, not long behind the prospectors and miners. So it was that within a year of the Mammoth Mining Company's incorporation, Buck was writing from Mammoth City that "the main street here is a jam of men and teams coming in from all parts and loaded with every conceivable article." About his own ventures he enthused:

I am building a hotel, 21 x 40, two stories. Have it rented for 150 dollars per month. The man paid the rent when I commenced. You, living in one of those old built-up towns where it takes a year to build a house, know but little about a new mining town out here. My house will be finished in ten days after I start in and I think it would astonish you to live with us awhile and see how we live. But there is an excitement about this, building up new towns, that I like better than plodding along at some steady business. (25 May 1879)

Buck's Standard Hotel, perhaps named after the famous Standard Mine in Bodie, was reported to be one of the better ones in town. When it was completed, he leased a portion of it to R. T. Trigg. By August 6 the *Herald* observed that "a saw mill, blacksmith shops, stores, saloons, feed stable, etc. are here in running order." A subsequent article boasted of six hotels, six general stores and twenty-two saloons. If these numbers seem to indicate a large town, remember that "a ten-foot-square tent or shack plus a barrel of whisky and a few glasses were all that was needed to make a 'saloon'" (Smith 1976). The town even had a "photographic gallery" operated by Alfred McMillan. He stood ready, according to his business card in the November 22 *Herald*, "to catch your shadow ere the substance fades." Chalfant, in describing the euphoria that pervaded the camps, noted that by 1879 town lots with twenty-five foot frontage were selling for $1500. A full account of Mill City and Mammoth City appeared in the 3 January 1880 *Herald:*

About one-half mile further up the hill, approached by a good road, we come to Mill City. Here the Mammoth Mining Company have their forty-stamp mill and offices. There is one store, one hotel, one livery stable and several beautiful cottages occupied by the families of the employees of the mill. Still another half mile is to be traveled to reach the town proper, or Mammoth City. Here we find a well built town of some four or five hundred inhabitants. The houses are of a similar but better character than those usually found in new mining camps, and in order that the outside reader may form some idea of its extent, we give the following business resumé: Five large general merchandise houses; two hardware, tinware and stove establishments; three hotels; five restaurants and boarding houses; two barber shops; one bath house; four lodging houses; three livery stables; two breweries; two bakeries; twelve saloons; two billiard halls; two public halls; two drug stores; two news depots; one circulating library; one blacksmith and wagon shop; one millinery store; one cigar and fancy goods store; two butchers: two semi-weekly newspapers; two white and the usual number of Chinese laundries; sundry opium dens and one well built jail. Our town authorities consist of two Justices and two Constables, one Deputy Sheriff, one Night Watchman and Deputy Constable. There are numerous carpenters and other mechanics, and the general population is made up of miners and families, there being about sixty ladies and seventy-five children. The town has been singularly free from lawless characters, and is remarkable for the peace-loving and quiet character of its citizens.

Pine City

Half a mile up the road from Mammoth City lay Pine City (also known as Lake City). It has long been a puzzle. Its location was uncertain, almost gypsy-like; its road obscure; and repeated references to pasture and a meadow have been baffling because today all is dense forest. Some local history buffs doubted that Pine City ever existed at all. Some, including Adele Reed in her book *Old Mammoth,* have drawn maps with Pine City on Lake Mary's east shore. Several old maps, including the one on pp. 14–15, also show Pine City on the east shore. However, I have been unable to find any evidence of cabins or foundations there, either on shore or in the lake shallows. (The lake then was several feet lower.) You will find Pine City correctly located on the map on p. 45.

Using 1879–80 accounts, in 1965 I located not only Pine City—foundations, an arrastre, and livery stable artifacts—but also the undisturbed Pine City dump. At that time I reported the find to the Forest Service, for appropriate excavation and preservation. To my sorrow, nothing was done and the dump was vandalized and looted in the late '60s. Subsequently I located the approximate town boundaries, the axis of the road through Pine City, and the semi-circle of cabins at its upper end that took advantage of full sun and proximity to the freight road. Although Stephen Willard reported several miners' cabins close to the lake shore, most of Pine City lay on either side of the Fresno Flats toll road. Helen Doyle corroborates this location in her book *A Child Went Forth*. Telling of a visit in 1888 with Old Charley, a miner, she recalled that "all along the neglected road [between Mammoth City and Pine City] there were old log cabins, some with roofs caved in and meadow grass growing around them as though no paths had ever led to their doors."

Pine City, like Mineral Park, never did rise above satellite status to Mammoth City. Firewood cut from the surrounding area was stored there; its livery stable served the trans-Sierra saddle trains; and perhaps it also served as the residence for the Lisbon's miners. But Pine City is best remembered as the picnic area for all the district's residents. To accommodate them Jerry (Jeremiah) McCarthy, a 34-year-old Irishman, and his 22-year-old brother opened a saloon and dancing pavilion on the shore of Lake Mary. For many years I was intrigued by the newspaper accounts of McCarthy's saloon, although many people dismissed them or argued for a location that made no sense from an 1880 perspective. In July 1985 I finally located the site, but until it has been properly excavated and preserved, I must decline to publish the location.

The camp's only street was Lake Avenue, which most likely was a portion of the toll road that went through Pine City. Beyond Pine City it narrowed to a trail—the trans-Sierra toll trail that led west across the Sierra to the San Joaquin Valley foothills, an important

A trace of the old wagon road from Mammoth City to Pine City. It was parallel to and west of today's Lake Mary Road.

freight and passenger route. Based upon my investigations between 1970 and '73, I determined that after leaving Mammoth City the road climbed southwest, more or less parallel with the present Lake Mary Road. It passed in front of several cabins, each with a rock-lined foundation, passed the Pine City Feed and Livery Stable (site of the present Mammoth Lakes Pack Outfit) and then swung northwest heading for Mammoth Pass. I found nine cabin foundations along this old road, all of them dating from the 1880 mining period. Three of the foundations are in line, 150 feet apart, and are the same distance from the road; they seem to be on measured lots. During one of my interviews with the late Beatrice Willard, she said very firmly that in 1924 there were "about a dozen cabins" in Pine City—standing structures, not just holes in the ground. Her husband Stephen had photographed several of them. By the 1950s the structures had collapsed, by the '60s most of the timbers had been carried away, and by now most of the sites have been vandalized, dug up, looted and all but obliterated.

The Pine City Feed and Livery Stable advertised its corral and pasture, as well as hay and grain for sale. This and many other references to a pasture have long been troubling, for today the Pine City area is a dense stand of lodgepole pine. Old Charley, the miner who is the central figure in chapter five, refers to a meadow repeatedly: "There's plenty of grass in the meadows for Jinny and Joan.... Now I'll go up and turn them out on the meadow...." (Doyle 1935). Where is this meadow? What has happened to it? Except for small grassy patches here and there, today no meadows occur anywhere in the lakes basin. Interviews with the Willards, and others' accounts, confirm that in the 1920s and '30s the area south of the present Pack Outfit was open, grassy, well-watered and relatively free of timber. Since this area today has a dense stand of young trees all about the same age, one can reasonably argue that they got their start in a meadow, which would foster such dense seeding. Perhaps this was a natural meadow or, more likely, a meadow that developed after trees were cut during the first years of Lake District. The few photographs of this area taken around the 1920s show many young trees among a few larger ones. Doyle's remark, that "the flat that we saw covered with the new growth of pine and fir trees had been a clearing, where there were cabins and stores...." (1935), indicates that in the late 1880s a new forest was already beginning to take hold.

The 1880 census for Pine City lists a total population of seventeen, including four housewives, three blacksmiths, two miners, and one each laborer, toll road operator, engineer and grocer. Of the six blacksmiths in Lake District, three of them lived in Pine City. They would have been busy taking care of French's saddle trains, working at the livery stable and building and repairing sleds and equipment for hauling wood. "Pine City is destined...to become a town of some importance...." proclaimed the *Herald* in July of 1879. But Pine City never fulfilled that prediction and a year later the same paper observed somberly that "a few scattered cabins and Jerry McCarthy's saloon was the sum total of improvements in Pine City" (7 April 1880).

LAKE DISTRICT
GHOST TOWNS TODAY

The map on the opposite page shows today's place names and today's roads. The location for Pine City has been confirmed by the author's archaeological investigations. Red Mountain is today's name for Mineral Hill.

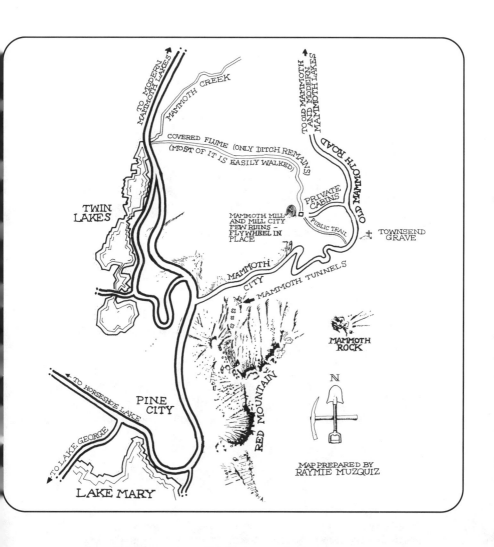

TO MODERN MAMMOTH LAKES

MAMMOTH CREEK

TO OLD MAMMOTH AND MODERN MAMMOTH LAKES

OLD MAMMOTH ROAD

COVERED FLUME (ONLY DITCH REMAINS)
(MOST OF IT IS EASILY WALKED)

TWIN LAKES

PRIVATE CABINS

MAMMOTH MILL AND MILL CITY FEW RUINS – FLYWHEEL IN PLACE

PUBLIC TRAIL

TOWNSEND GRAVE

MAMMOTH CITY

MAMMOTH TUNNELS

MAMMOTH ROCK

N

RED MOUNTAIN

TO HORSESHOE LAKE

PINE CITY

TO LAKE GEORGE

LAKE MARY

MAP PREPARED BY
RAYMIE MUZQUIZ

STAMP-MILL OPERATION

The drawings that follow illustrate the general principles of stamp-mill operation. Some of the Mammoth mill's methods, explained in the text, differ a bit from the operations of the mills pictured. In fact, there are no detailed records of the Mammoth's milling methods. Both drawings are from the *Eighth Annual Report of the State Mineralogist,* 1888.

Cross-section of a gold mill. Ore entering the upper floor of a stamp mill was dropped over a large grate called a grizzly (top level, left), which sorted the rock. The finer ore fell into the ore bins, while the coarser went first to a crusher and then to the bins. From the bins (middle level), the ore was fed through gates to the batteries. The batteries pulverized the ore, reducing it to pulp, which then flowed across silver-plated copper plates (aprons) that had been coated with a thin layer of mercury. (The aprons at the Mammoth mill probably were unplated copper.) Some of the gold and silver combined with the mercury to form amalgam. The amalgam and pulp flowed down to the concentrators (lower level), which separated the gold- and silver-bearing mercury from the waste. The mill's power came from water wheels (lower right); note the series of belts and wheels that transferred power from them to all levels of the mill.

Cutaway of a gold mill. This drawing shows how a mill should be sited. Ideally it should have 40 feet of fall from the ore bins at the top to the concentrators at the bottom. Gravity thus becomes the powerful force that drops the ore from level to level within the mill. Additionally, it should be located "in close proximity to, but below the level of, the collar of the shaft or the mouth of the tunnel, on sloping ground, where the ore can be delivered directly from the mine to a 'grizzly' on the upper floor of the mill...." *(California Gold Mill Practices* 1895). In the engine room (lowest level) are three water wheels, driven by water under pressure. On the right is a six-foot Knight wheel (like the Mammoth mill), which powered the batteries. In the center, a four-foot Pelton (?) wheel that drove the crushers. On the left, a three-foot wheel that ran the concentrators.

Chapter 5 ☙

PINE CITY TALES

Fifteen-year-old Helen MacKnight (Doyle) spent the summer of
1888 with her friends Frances and Grace on their families' ranches
in Long Valley. The stories about Old Charley and Pine City that
follow are from her autobiography, *A Child Went Forth,* an honest
and vivid portrayal of eastern Sierra frontier life and its people as
she knew them from 1887 to 1917. As an adult, Helen practiced
medicine in Bishop, married and raised her family there. Among
those she always remembered was a miner known as Old Charley,
whom she met that summer in Long Valley.

> One day when Grace and Frances and I were sitting on the long
> porch wondering what to do...we heard a tinkle of bells and looked
> up the road to see two tired but determined-looking burros coming
> toward us.... They suddenly stopped to grab a bite of the bunch
> grass that grew by the roadside. Then Old Charley appeared.
>
> As soon as I saw him I thought of a pine tree, standing on
> some ridge. I had seen them with their trunks bare and curved to
> the prevailing wind, and with all their branches reaching to the
> storm-sheltered valley below. Old Charley's frame was bent the
> same way. His arms were long and his hands big and gnarled look-
> ing, and as much of his face as could be seen above his long,
> sparse beard was burned and wrinkled like the red lava wash on
> the side of a crater. His blue eyes shone from that setting with the
> same startling contrast as a blue mountain lake set in an old crater

bed. His nose was hooked and pushed to one side, as if he had run into something in a blinding storm. His eyes mirrored the kindliest possible smile, as he indulgently left the burros to enjoy the sweet, juicy bunch grass....

"I'm headin' for Pine City," he said in answer to our questions. "Used to mine there when the boom was on. When it petered out I took Jinny and Joan [his burros] and started travelin'. We've been a lot o' places.... But I'm a rock man. Washin' sand don't interest me. I'm gettin' along, an' all the time I was travelin' round I kep' thinkin' of Old Pine City an' Lake Mary. I hain't seen as purty a place anywhere as that is.

Helen describes what they found at Pine City a few weeks later when they rode horseback to visit him:

In a grove of firs we saw a well preserved cabin and there were evidences about the place that Old Charley had taken up his abode there.

It was the prettiest spot imaginable. Wild roses blossomed on bushes that grew behind the cabin where the sandy hillside started up from the meadow. There were red columbine along a stream that gurgled by. Pine birds, deep blue as a shadowed mountain lake, flew from tamarack to fir and pine trees....

We heard a clatter of loose rocks and looked up. Jinny and Joan, with Old Charley behind them, were coming down a trail that led from the mouth of a tunnel high up on the mountain side.

We rode across the meadow to meet them. Old Charley seemed happy and Jinny and Joan were sleek and fat and had lost that determined look. Their kyaxes [kyack, a packsack that hangs on either side of a packsaddle] were filled to bulging with rock. They were on the way to the arastra, and we went along. Old Charley had dug a round pit, deep enough so that the top came to my waist when I stood in it, and twice as far across as I could reach.

The bottom was of large, flat rocks and Old Charley showed us how he had left big cracks between and filled them in so that they were still below the surface of the rocks. He poured quicksilver into these cracks. Then he emptied the kyaxes into the pit. He hitched Jinny and Joan to the tamarack sweep from which other flat rocks were suspended, so that the ore would be ground between them and the rocks on the bottom of the pit. He turned in a stream of water that he had brought from the creek which ran near the cabin, and started Jinny and Joan pulling the sweep around the pit. There was a great commotion as rock attacked rock, and Old Charley said the quartz would be ground to powder

A water-powered arrastre is a simple machine for crushing ore. Old Charley's arrastre, described in this chapter, was powered by his two burros.

In the 1890s, according to the *Ninth Report of the State Mineralogist*, there were perhaps "one hundred arrastras running in different parts of the State, some of them by water, the greater number, however, by horse or mule power. The latter crush an average of one ton, and the former two to three tons per day. These machines are employed where there is only a small amount of ore to be crushed, and which must necessarily be of good grade to justify its being worked by this slow method. The arrastra process is a favorite one with the Mexicans, in whose country it is largely adopted in both gold and silver mining" (California State Mining Bureau, 1890).

Two views of the water wheel that powered an arrastre near upper Pine City.

Photo (right) by Robert D. Jones, 1922. Martha Wynne collection

A dragstone from a Pine City arrastre. Dragged around and around the arrastre's circular rock structure, two or four heavy dragstones crushed the ore into pieces small enough that the gold and silver could be separated out. Arrastres were powered by mules, burros, horses or water wheels.

and the gold would be grabbed by the quicksilver that lay in the cracks, to form amalgam. A stream began to flow from a pipe on the down hillside to a muddy mass that Old Charley said was the tailings pond.

We left Jinny and Joan plodding round and round the circle, as though they had never dreamed of bunch grass. Old Charley told us where to find a wild strawberry patch, and said he would make a short cake and we would have a picnic....

When we returned, there was a fire going in the ruins of an old fireplace where a cabin had once stood. Old Charley was making frying-pan bread, and trout that he had caught in Lake Mary that morning were sizzling over the fire. They were so fresh that they squirmed in the bacon grease in which he cooked them. We had a stump for a table and rocks for chairs. The frying-pan bread was cut through the middle and the mashed berries put between the crisp layers. Old Charley brought dishes and beans from his cabin. He said no miner's meal was complete without beans. That was the kind of picnic one never forgets!

While he ate Old Charley told us of the time when Pine City had been a camp of ten thousand people [a sizeable exaggeration, no doubt inspired by three gullible young girls]. There had been Fourth of July celebrations on Lake Mary, and the flat that we saw covered with the new growth of pine and fir trees had been a clearing where there were cabins and stores and saloons and gambling houses. [Already the stories are drifting away from fact toward romance.]

Then we went to look at Old Charley's cabin. There was one room, built of logs, and a lean-to shed-kitchen. A rough pine bedstead stood in one corner, and a wood box as big as the bed hugged the fireplace. There was a pine table with the top worn smooth and so soaked with bacon grease that it looked as if it had been rubbed with wax. There were shelves with mining supplies and a black kettle with a spout, which Old Charley said was a retort. The fireplace was wide enough to take great pine logs.

Old Charley said he had found everything in the cabin. The wood box was even filled with logs.

While Jinny and Joan continued working at the arrastre, Charley turned to story telling—spicing his tales with his own philosophy and, at the same time, providing a great deal of insight into the heartbreak, broken dreams and tragedy that were all too commonplace in a miner's life.

While Old Charley smoked his corn-cob pipe, he told us more about Pine City in the days when he was a young man.

"You know," he said, "folks shake the dust of a busted mining town like rats desert a sinking ship. They walk out an' leave everything, furniture and beds an' dishes on the table, maybe, like they had et an' run. I suppose that's the reason they got the name of 'ghost towns'.

"When the mines are running and freight teams hauling ore an' bullion out, it's easy enough to get in furniture an' fixin's, an' some of these cabins was done up real purty. Men had their families come an' the wimmen put paper on the walls an' lace curtains at the windows. An' then the mines closed down in the fall an' every one ran like scared coyotes to get out before the snows came."

Mary Townsend's Grave

Old Charley then related the tragedy that took the life of Mary Townsend (Mrs. J. E.) in November 1881. She was thirty-four years old. He was an eyewitness, and his story has been corroborated by Townsend family members.

"There was a fellow in camp that had been a kind of pardner of mine, off an' on, up around Feather River and over in Nevada, in early days on the Comstock. He'd got married an' brought his wife up to the camp at Pine City.

"We thought we had a lead in a tunnel that looked as though it might break into a pocket any time, an' we decided to hole in for the winter an' maybe do a little work if the snow wasn't too heavy, an' be here on the job when spring broke.

"He'd ought to have sent his wife out, but she was a purty thing an' they was terribly in love. She was young an' strong an' was all for stayin' an' spendin' the winter with us. We had one of the biggest storms I ever saw in these mountains an' before it stopped the snow was six feet on the level and drifted over the roofs of the cabins in lots of places. The nearest settlement was a hundred miles away an' there wasn't any way to get out except by snow-shoes.

"One day my pardner and I thought we'd go out an' kill some snow-shoe rabbits an' have some fresh meat. We were cleanin' our shot guns an' somehow a shell got jammed in my pardner's gun barrel, an' while he was tryin' to get it out the gun went off an' shot his wife.

"I've been through some bad times in rip-roarin' mining camps, but never anything like that. My pardner was beside himself. I was afraid to leave him alone a minute. We couldn't bury his wife. There was no place to dig a grave. All we could do was to make a hole in the snow an' keep her there till spring.

"He wouldn't go away an' leave her. At first he raved like a maniac. Then he took sick an' I had to nurse him an' keep drivin' new stakes in the snow that kept driftin', so as we could find her body in the spring before the coyotes did.

"My pardner got well after a while an' when the snow melted off on the flat down there we took his wife down and buried her. She came from back East an' she had always dreamed of havin' a house with a picket fence around it, so nothin' would do but we must put a picket fence around her grave. It took us quite a while to do it with the tools we had, but we did a good job. I was noticin' the other day, that fence is just as strong an' straight as 'twas when we put it there. [Her grave, now fenced with heavy boards, is beside the Old Mammoth Road. The picket fence replacements were stolen repeatedly.]

"My pardner an' I moved into another cabin and started workin' the tunnel in the spring [this came to be known as the Albright tunnel], but all the deserted cabins, with the dishes on the tables an' maybe a baby's crib or a rag doll lyin' around, got on our nerves an' we left to find new diggin's."

Old Charley's story seemed to bring back the shades of all those people who had made the shores of Lake Mary echo to their voices. We felt as though he had forgotten us, but he reassured us with his kindly smile and continued: "You know, I felt mighty bad at the time all this happened but I came to see that maybe it was for the best. That little woman was taken when she was soft an' warm an' care-free an' gay as a kitten, dreamin' of her little home with a picket fence.

"There's nothin' more forlorn than a woman in a minin' camp longin' for back home. The mountain peaks and the forests get to be walls holdin' 'em back an' keepin' 'em from gettin' where they want to go. They just can't see a view or a beautiful sunset for the Down East frame houses an' picket fences that get in their way."

Who Was Old Charley?

References to Old Charley have haunted me for years. Just who was he? Finally, after piecing together bits of evidence and clues from several sources, I feel confident that he was Dewitt C. Albright, listed in the 1880 census of Mammoth City as age 50 from New York. That he chose to use his middle instead of his first name is not unusual. (I go by my middle name, as did my father before me.) It was widely known that a Charley Albright had a mine at the base of Mineral Hill, not far from the water-powered arrastre at the upper end of Pine City. He had his own arrastre farther across the meadow. Tom Rigg, in a letter to Adele Reed (1982), says that Charlie Albright worked at the mines during the boom days and that later, in 1892, he and Albright lived in a cabin in Pine City. The Albright tunnel still exists, all 236 feet of it—including one drift, and track on all but the last forty-seven feet. The last work in the Albright occurred during 1939 and 1940, when A. E. Beauregard, his two brothers and A. E.'s 13-year-old son, Don, dug the last twenty feet, prepared the wall for the next blast and then walked away, having found a more promising ledge elsewhere on Red Mountain.

Frasher Collection, Pomona Public Library. Print courtesy of USFS, Inyo National Forest.
Pine City miner's cabin c. 1920, along the road from Mammoth City.

A Melancholy Exile

Old Charley was typical of many a prospector, but not all ghost-camp miners were as serene and content as he. Among Tuolumne miners, Mark Twain found instead only unbearable melancholy:

> By and by, an old friend of mine, a miner, came down from one of the decayed mining camps of Tuolumne, California, and I went back with him. We lived in a small cabin on a verdant hillside, and there were not five other cabins in view over the wide expanse of hill and forest. Yet a flourishing city of two or three thousand population had occupied this grassy dead solitude during the flush times of twelve or fifteen years before, and where our cabin stood had once been the heart of the teeming hive, the center of the city. When the mines gave out the town fell into decay, and in a few years wholly disappeared—streets, dwellings, shops, everything—and left no sign. The grassy slopes were as green and smooth and desolate of life as if they had never been disturbed. The mere handful of miners still remaining had seen the town spring up, spread, grow, and flourish in its pride; and they had

Pine City miner's cabin, 1922. Martha Wynne at the window.

Photo by Robert D. Jones, Martha Wynne collection

seen it sicken and die, and pass away like a dream. With it their hopes had died, and their zest of life. They had long ago resigned themselves to their exile.... They had accepted banishment, forgotten the world and been forgotten of the world. They were far from telegraphs and railroads, and they stood, as it were, in a living grave, dead to the events that stirred the globe's great populations...isolated and out cast.... It was the most singular, and almost the most touching and melancholy exile that fancy can imagine. (Clemens 1872)

Contentment and One Man Who Found It

But the word *exile* does not fit Old Charley at all. He had decided to stay for the winter because he wanted "to work those old tunnels an' settle down to rest an' ruminate. I know there ain't nobody there any more, but there's some old cabins an' I can always take out enough rock to keep me in beans an' bacon, an' there's plenty of grass in the meadows for Jinny an' Joan."

As the girls were saying good-by to Charley, they suddenly realized that the sound of breaking rock and slushing water from the arrastre had stopped.

"Well," Old Charley explained, "Jinny an' Joan have just decided that they're through for today. I never argue with them. When they're through, they're through an' that's all there is to it. But they always play fair an' get a lot done before they quit. Now I'll go up and turn them out on the meadow, an' you best be makin' tracks for home."

No, not exile and not melancholy here. Out of his arrastre Old Charley could get enough to buy beans and bacon, flour and coffee for the winter; and he could cut grass on the upper meadow to make hay for Jinny and Joan. His self-sufficiency, along with Jinny and Joan's companionship, reveal instead a man living where he wanted to live and making his living in the way he wanted. A man who knew what contentment was and where to find it.

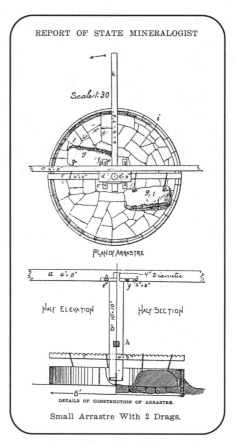

Scale 1:30

PLAN OF ARRASTRE

HALF ELEVATION   HALF SECTION

DETAILS OF CONSTRUCTION OF ARRASTRE.

Small Arrastre With 2 Drags.

Report of State Mineralogist XXX, 1934

Chapter 6

WAGON ROADS & PACK TRAILS

Lake District was far from everywhere. The first prospectors came on foot or on horseback; there was no other way. No wagon roads, only trails led to the nearest mining camps, Bodie and Benton, and to the ranching town of Bishop Creek. The nearest rail head was 150 miles north at Carson City, on the Virginia & Truckee Railway. It, in turn, connected with the Central Pacific Rail Road at Reno. Mojave, on the Southern Pacific Railway, was 220 long hot miles south. How were the mines and miners to obtain all the things they needed—the heavy milling machinery, track and ore cars; clothing, tools, medicines and food; horses, mules, hay and grain? Where was it all to come from? And how?

As it turned out, whenever a new camp needed something— cattle, flour, lumber or wagon roads—no matter how isolated that camp might be, some enterprising person always showed up to provide it. Someone always managed to bring in freight wagons or pack trains loaded with supplies. Sometimes wagons could make their own routes and, with use, those routes became rough but passable roads. But where rough, difficult terrain required road-work, someone built a road and charged toll.

Connections North and East: Roads to Benton and Bodie

A. C. Webster constructed a wagon road east to Benton, a silver camp forty-eight miles distant and an important link with the railroads to the north. From Casa Diablo the road headed across Long Valley and forded the Owens River at Benton Crossing (the old crossing is now under Crowley Lake). Stages and freight wagons from the rail head at Carson City regularly plied the 150 miles to Benton, and coaches clattered back and forth between Benton and Mammoth City three times a week, bringing mail and passengers. From Carson City via Benton came livestock, shipments of produce, goods for the retail stores, and supplies for the restaurants and saloons. From Benton, bullion was shipped to the U.S. Mint in Carson City or in San Francisco.

Bodie, a famous gold and silver camp northeast of Mono Lake, also provided a link to Carson City and the railroads to the north. Con Ogg of Mammoth City instituted the Lake and Bodie Stage Line, with an office in the Monumental Hotel. The stage line schedule, as set forth in the 25 October 1879 *Mammoth City Herald,* listed a daily departure at 4:00 a.m. and a twelve-dollar fare for the twelve-hour trip. Later the fare was increased to fifteen dollars and departures reduced to Mondays, Thursdays and Saturdays. In its 6 December 1879 issue, the *Mammoth City Times* advertised:

LAKE AND BODIE STAGE LINE
Carrying U. S. Mails and Wells, Fargo & Co.'s Express.
Stages leave Mammoth City for King's Ranch and Bodie,
Sundays, Wednesdays and Fridays. At 4 a.m.
Time to Bodie, Where Close Connection is Made with the Carson
Stage Line, Twelve Hours.
Fare to Bodie, $15

The *Herald* for 13 September reported that Con Ogg's stages had carried "from 300 to 500 pounds of mail matter every stage trip for nothing," although he did not have a mail contract with the federal government. (These numbers seem large, considering Lake District's population.) Apparently feeling this to be more of a public charity than he could continue, not to mention the wear and tear on his animals and equipment, Ogg announced that beginning

Wagons similar to this one hauled supplies across the desert to Lake District from Carson City, Benton, Bishop Creek and Mojave. Note the iron-tired wheels and the wooden brake shoe.

October first, 1879, he would operate under the same stipulations as Wells, Fargo & Company, that the postage rate would be five cents a letter, and that mail would depart for Bodie every Wednesday, Friday and Sunday. He expected to continue service in winter, using mule-drawn sleighs and mail carriers on skis (known then as *snowshoes*). Ogg planned to pasture his horses at lower elevations for the winter and to store his wagons and coaches in sheds. Travel to and from Lake District generally followed this seasonal pattern. As winter approached, horses were taken to lower altitudes, wagons were stored, and sleighs and sleds were readied for the coming snow.

Freight from the north also came through Bodie, where it was usually transferred to George S. Elder's Fast Freight Line. An ad for the company in the 19 November 1879 *Times* listed the following freight rates: for barley and flour, $2 per 100 pounds; for general merchandise, hardware, machinery and malt, $2.25 per 100 pounds; for furniture, fruits, vegetables and all consignments of less than 500 pounds, $2.75 per 100 pounds. Outgoing freight departed Mammoth City at 5:00 a.m. and each item to be shipped had to be marked "Elder's Fast Freight." From Bodie, shipments to Carson City took three days; return shipments left Carson City every other day at 5:00 A.M.

Connections South: Jim Sherwin's Toll Road to Bishop Creek

Pioneer settlers in Round Valley and Bishop Creek, at the northern end of Owens Valley, sorely needed lumber. The nearest trees were miles away, high up steep mountain slopes. In order to supply lumber to Owens Valley, in the early 1870s J. L. C. Sherwin built a road from Owens Valley north into Rock Creek Canyon, to the saw mill of his associates, James and Joseph Rowin. From Bishop Creek (now Bishop) to Round Valley was a relatively easy 15-mile haul—sandy in spots but flat. But an abrupt 3,000-foot-high volcanic flow bounds Round Valley on the north. To reach Rock Creek, Sherwin built a wagon road part way up that slope. It bears his name still, Sherwin Grade.

When Lake District boomed, Sherwin extended his wagon road

Wagon tracks, cut into the soft volcanic rock on Sherwin Grade north of Bishop, mark the Sherwin toll road to Mammoth City. After more than a hundred years, here and there in the brush it is still recognizable.

to the top of the grade and then on to Lake District, making it possible to travel the forty miles between Mammoth City and Round Valley in a single day—though a very long, grueling day. His toll road provided an important link with the Southern Pacific Railway at Mojave, 220 miles to the south. Sherwin initially selected a route that required little blasting, a route that favored the slope's contours, but near the summit heavy wagons sank to their axles in soft sand. He then rerouted the upper portion, making cuts into the soft volcanic rock. This new route resulted in surer footing for the struggling animals and considerably less swearing for the teamsters. He later sold his road to the Dickinson brothers, who improved it further. West of today's four-lane highway up Sherwin Grade, you can still find remnants of Sherwin's road and the ruts made by countless iron-tired wagon wheels.

But Sherwin Grade, even with improvements, was always a difficult haul. Stage passengers got out and walked and often pushed. In his *Tales of the Pioneers,* W. A. Chalfant related that "when the huge flywheel for the mill was being transported in sections by a freighting team, it fell from the top of Sherwin Hill road and crashed to the bottom of the canyon, eight hundred feet below." This story needs a bit of unscrambling. First of all, it is true that the flywheel was shipped in sections—by sea from Belgium where it was cast, then by rail and by wagon to Mill City where the sections were assembled. Secondly, according to Remi Nadeau, it was not a section of the flywheel that rolled down Sherwin Grade but the huge boiler for the steam plant. (Author Nadeau is the namesake and great-great–grandson of the famous wagon freighter who dominated the freight traffic in southern and eastern California from 1869 to 1882.)

> In hauling in machinery for the stamp mill, the huge boiler offered the toughest problem. It was carried by rail from San Francisco to Mojave, then carefully transferred to one of Nadeau's twenty-mule-team freight wagons. Then for 10 or 12 days it was pulled across the Mojave Desert and through Owens Valley.
>
> Finally, the plodding animals reached Sherwin Grade—a day's haul from Mammoth City. As they labored upward to the tune of cracking blacksnake and jingling chains, the wagon toppled over

and the boiler crashed into the canyon below. No amount of straining and swearing could haul the stubborn object back up the road, and at last report it lay there still.

This incident must have occurred in 1879, while the mill was shut down for alterations. Nadeau goes on to say:

> ...clearly painted on the [fly] wheel in two places are the letters: "M.M. Co., Care of C.G.F. Co., Mojave." This forwarding address marked there by a Southern Pacific Railroad freight agent may be translated: "Mammoth Mining Company, Care of Cerro Gordo Freighting Company, Mojave"—the latter being the freighting outfit operated by Remi Nadeau....(1965)

Connections West:
J. S. French's Toll Trail to Fresno Flats

A wagon road west over the rugged Sierra Nevada was out of the question, but J. S. French pioneered a saddle trail. It led from Pine City to Fresno Flats (now Oakhurst, 46 miles north of Fresno) in the western Sierra foothills. Passengers, all manner of freight, produce, livestock (including sheep), and even some mining equipment came from the San Joaquin Valley to Mammoth City over this trail. Fresno Flats also provided important connections with the stages for Madera and San Francisco. The 30 July 1879 *Herald* ran these two ads for the saddle train to Fresno Flats:

> LAKE DISTRICT AND FRESNO FLATS SADDLE TRAIN.
> Leaves Mammoth City Tuesdays and Fridays at 5 a.m.
> Leaves Fresno Flats same days on arrival of the Madera stages.
> Twenty pounds of baggage free.
> Freight from Fresno Flats to Mammoth 8¢.
> *Fare to Fresno Flats, $15.00 Fare to Madera, $20.00*
> *Fare to San Francisco, $29.00*

> THE MONUMENTAL HOTEL, CENTRAL MAMMOTH AVENUE,
> The Leading Hotel of Mammoth City.
> This hotel is the headquarters of San Francisco and Bodie travel, and is first class in every respect.
> *The Fresno Flats saddle train arrives and departs from our door.*

According to an unpublished manuscript belonging to A. E. Beauregard, "French's saddle trains met the Yosemite stages at Fresno

Flats and traveled to Beasore Meadows, Reds Meadow, through Mammoth Pass and then to Mammoth City, a distance of 54 miles." Two contemporary comments indicate that this was a long, hard ride. The first, by one of its correspondents, appeared on the front page of the *Daily Alta California:* "Our trail went up one backbone after another, every succeeding one higher than the one before" (24 July 1879). The other comes from the July 30 *Herald:* "Charlie Ratcliffe arrived from San Francisco last night by the Fresno Flat route. To-day Mr. Ratcliffe is knocking about, but it is manifest that he has a tender regard for the seat of his trowsers."

The Difficulties in Locating Old Roads

So much has vanished since Lake District's heyday that it is often difficult—sometimes impossible—to locate old roads and structures. Everything that could be used has been hauled away—lumber, shingles, tools, scrap metal. Fire and snow have demolished what was left. Many sites have been bulldozed and vandalized; others are overgrown with brush.

Perhaps you would be interested in the methods I used to locate the Fresno Flats Road, for it was not recognizable. Since it is mining camp custom to build cabins along roads (confirmed by Helen Doyle in her description of Pine City), I started by plotting the extant cabin foundations from a known point on the old auto road to Lake Mary. They curved in a semi-circle below the present Lake Mary Road. Interviews with the Willards confirmed my findings. With this general indication of where the road might have gone, I photographed the area using black-and-white film in oblique sunlight. This took much persistence, for Red Mountain blocks the morning light and dense trees block much of the afternoon light. But eventually I had a series of photos in which shadows, thrown by the oblique light, revealed surface features of the old wagon road that were not visible to the eye. I could locate no trace of the road beyond Lake Mamie's outlet; but then that was to be expected, for the wagon road reportedly narrowed to a saddle trail shortly after leaving Pine City.

Chapter 7

LAKE DISTRICT'S PEOPLE

Pinpointing population numbers for old mining camps is just about impossible. From winter to summer and from one year to the next, numbers could increase ten- or twenty-fold, and then decrease just as quickly. However, the 1880 census gives us firm figures for June of that year and there are some reasonable estimates for prior years in Lake District.

In June of 1878, shortly after General Dodge founded the Mammoth Mining Company, the estimated population was 125 persons, excluding Indians. Probably the highest numbers occurred the following summer; during the flush year of 1879 perhaps 2500 gold hunters thronged the district. But Chalfant qualifies this claim: "To make up this number, transients in and out of the surrounding districts of Prescott, Mountain View, Laurel and North Fork were included in the enumeration" (1935). Few stayed on, however; during the winter of 1879–80, Mammoth City reportedly had a "permanent" population of 400 or 500. The 1880 census, taken between June 8 and June 24 when snow lay on the ground and the mill was still shut down, gives a population of 610 for the district including Pine City and Mineral Park, each of which contributed seventeen souls to the total. This is probably the minimum number for the summer of 1880. It is likely that during July and August others

States and Territories of Origin
Lake District Residents, 1880 Census

California	98	Maryland	2	Ohio	25
Connecticut	1	Massachusetts	10	Oregon	1
Georgia	1	Michigan	7	Pennsylvania	16
Idaho Territory	2	Missouri	10	Tennessee	8
Illinois	17	Minnesota	1	Texas	4
Indiana	5	Mississippi	2	Utah	1
Iowa	11	Montana Terr.	1	Vermont	4
Kansas	7	Nevada	22	Washington Terr.	1
Kentucky	8	New Hampshire	4	Wisconsin	6
Louisiana	2	New Jersey	6	Wyoming Territory	2
Maine	9	New York	46		

drifted in, but by the next winter of 1880–81 the district's population was declining rapidly. Old Charley's memories of 10,000 people can be dismissed as gross exaggeration for the sake of a good story; there is not a shred of evidence to support such numbers.

Whatever the exact numbers, Lake District experienced explosive growth during the boom years of 1878 and 1879. One indicator of this growth is the production of McFarland and Fraser's lumber mill. The *Engineering and Mining Journal* for July–December 1878 reported "10,000 feet of lumber per day" being produced by the newly-erected sawmill. By July first, 1879, according to Chalfant, the mill had produced 650,000 feet of lumber and the shingle mill had turned out 400,000 shingles.

Their Origins

Far more interesting than the numbers, however, is what the census tells us about the people—who they were, where they were from and what they did for a living. The census reveals some important characteristics of the people in Lake District. Reflecting the nearly eight million immigrants that entered America between 1851 and 1880, of

Cities, Provinces and Countries of Origin
Lake District Residents, 1880 Census

Austria	6	France	13	Nova Scotia	21
The Azores	2	Germany	2	Poland	1
Baden	1	Hamburg	1	Portugal	4
Bavaria	1	Hanover	5	Prince Edward Is.	6
Braunschweig	1	Hungary	2	Prussia	9
Canada	32	Ireland	59	Saxony	1
China	44	Luxemburg	1	Scotland	5
Dalmatia	1	Mecklingburg	3	Sweden	1
Denmark	1	Mexico	3	Switzerland	2
England	26	New Brunswick	3	Wales	3
Flores	1	Norway	5	Wirtemburg	1

Lake District's residents 270 or 44 percent were foreign-born. They represented 32 states or territories and 33 foreign locations.

Analysis of the census shows a population that was culturally but not racially diverse. There is no record at all of how many Paiute Indians were in Lake District. "Notwithstanding the cold weather the Piutes are still in town in considerable numbers, and they appear to be as happy as clams at high tide," observed the *Mammoth City Herald* on 22 November 1879. (Indians were not counted in the census because they were not considered citizens; the press had little to say concerning their status. The United States government maintained the legal fiction that Indian groups were separate nations with whom treaties could be made and from whom land cessions could be extracted.) Unsubstantiated accounts say that a few Paiutes were employed in the mines and that others worked for various townspeople. The *Herald* for 13 August 1879 noted that Indians caught trout on the South Fork of the San Joaquin River (Fish Creek), and Franklin Buck wrote that an "Indian Jim" was with him on a fishing trip to the South Fork. Indian Jim has sometimes been confused with another Paiute guide, Mono

Jim, who was killed in the 1871 shootout with six escaped convicts at Convict Lake.

While we don't know the peak Chinese population, the census shows seven percent: forty-four Chinese working as laundrymen, cooks, laborers, grocers, physicians, gardeners and prostitutes (five). The *Mammoth City Times* for 13 September 1879 noted a "Chinese wash house—near central portion of town." Amid solemn warnings about putting caps on the tall stove pipes that graced the roofs of tents and cabins, because "a conflagration may be expected at any time," the *Herald* aimed one of its warnings specifically at the Chinese: "Another opium den in course of construction right in the centre of town on Main street. There will be a big fire down there some of these windy days and clean them all out" (22 Nov. 1879).

But these fearful warnings about potential fire were wasted in the high mountain air. No one was too excited about uncapped stove pipes, including the Chinese who regarded their opium dens as a cultural tie to the Celestial Empire. The prevalent white attitude toward the Chinese is expressed in no uncertain terms in the 31 July 1880 *Herald:*

> English military critics believe that if the Chinese learn how to fight they will make a very dangerous people, because they are robust, temperate, obedient and have no fear of death. The Chinese are just like all mongrel and half-formed races. They can be taught perfect discipline and will fight so long as they are under the control of competent commanders, but once confused they are idiots.

Although today we are appalled by such racist statements, they expressed the general attitude in nineteenth century mining camps and were not considered out of the ordinary or in bad taste.

Their Families

Of the 610 people recorded by name, 146 or 24 percent were female; 464 were male. Ages ranged from two months to 81. Ninety-five of the females were between the ages of 18 and 76. The octogenarian was farmer Logan Shelton from Illinois; his 37-year-old wife Rebecca was from Iowa. She had two children, a girl 16 and a boy 14, and together they had two more, a son age 4 and a girl of 8 months. In those times, the Shelton's family was not considered a large one. Large families were desirable, both to offset the high infant mortality and to ensure more hands to help with farm work. Editor and publisher William Barnes also had four children. He was 50; his wife 30; and his four children ranged from 8 to 3 years old. Boarding-house keeper Samuel (age 36) and Mary (age 34) Argall of the Argall House had five children ranging from 13 years to 4 months. S. C. Sherwin, 54, a farmer from Ohio, and his 46-year-old wife Nancy from Kentucky had six children: four girls and two boys between 17 and 5 years old. T. H. Elliot, 42, owner of the Lake House, a hotel on lower Mammoth Avenue, and his 40-year-old wife were both from Pennsylvania and had seven children between 20 and 3 years old. Early marriages were common. Mary Dunn, age 22 and wife of 26-year-old Daniel Dunn, had an 8-year-old son, Otis. Ana Trigg, wife of 37-year-old R. J. Trigg, was 18 years old and had a son 2 years old. The 21-year-old wife of George Huckaby, age 21, had three children ranging from one to five years old. Rarely would women have a child late; however, Oliver Cromwell was listed as age 69, his wife 60, and their son 16.

The number of children recorded in the census, 105 or 17 percent of the total, is truly surprising. Thirty-one of them were between the ages of two months and three years; 74 were between four and seventeen years. The census noted that several seventeen-year-olds were apprenticed and not attending school. Despite the uncertainties of mining-camp life, it is evident that men did not hesitate to bring their wives and children to a new district and commit them to whatever future the mines and luck might bring.

Their Occupations

Life in Lake District was a far cry from the gold rush camps of 1849, which consisted primarily of young male Americans. Here were many foreign-born and many families with children. While conditions were still harsh, they were considerably better than the crude, makeshift living conditions endured by the forty-niners. And instead of every man for himself, panning gold on his own, here was a society that was economically complex and interdependent.

Some Occupations in Lake District
1880 Census

Miners	121	Hotel keepers	10	Engineers	5
Laborers	34	Prostitutes	7	Machinists	4
Housewives	31	Sheep raisers	7	Sawmill employees	3
Carpenters	18	Butchers	6	Stock raisers	3
Laundrymen	17	General merchants	6	Physician/surgeons	3
Cooks	15	Blacksmiths	6	Bookkeepers	3
Farmers	13	Boardinghs. keepers	5	Saloon keepers	3
Liquor dealers	10	Restaurant keepers	5	Grocers	3

Seventy-five different occupations were listed in the 1880 census, including housewives but excluding one "sailor."

Of the physicians two were Chinese, ages 53 and 50, and the other was Irish, Dr. P. J. Ragan. In addition to the occupations listed in the table above, there were two tinsmiths, brewers, liverymen, editors, teamsters, amalgamators, milliners, assayers, bakers, justices of the peace, constables, dressmakers, barbers, stonemasons, tailors, accountants, mining superintendents and lawyers. And one stonecutter, drug maker, postmaster, photographer, livery-stable keeper, shoemaker, toll-road keeper, wallpaperer, sawyer, huckster, lumber dealer, wheelwright, stage driver, clerk, stationer, mining recorder, policeman, barkeeper, printer, mining engineer, flume builder, street contractor, sawmill operator, mill worker, deputy sheriff, plasterer, landlord, landlady, engineer/surveyor, dentist, jeweler, painter and stage-station keeper.

Occupations listed in the census were only part of the picture, however. Thirty-eight-year-old D. J. MacDonald from Nova Scotia, for example, is listed as a miner, but he and a partner also rented out boats on Lake Mary. Given the low wages and the high cost of living, no doubt many others supplemented their income with part-time jobs. A full-time miner or carpenter might also be a woodcutter or boatbuilder on the side.

Chapter 8 ๑

ABOUT TOWN

Within a column headed "About Town," the *Mammoth City Times* disclosed anything and everything about anyone—from who had an unclaimed package at the stage office and the success of a local drama presentation to the contents of a consignment for the local cigar store. All aspects of life in Lake District were fair game to "About Town." For example:

Contracts were let for ashes for the toll road to cover it to prevent skidding.

Supt. Hardy returned from Bodie today, and in exactly two seconds by the watch, was astride his sorrel horse, flying around from pillar to post. The grass doesn't get...a chance to grow under Hardy's feet.

Another team of Nadeau's came in this afternoon. This is probably the last of the season.

The biggest wood pile in Pine City belongs to Hugh Glenn. Fortunately for him there are no houses near. *(Times* 19 Nov. 1879)

So, too, this chapter, like its 1879 namesake, will recount the stuff of everyday life in Lake District. How people lived, what things cost, why cash was scarce, what was important to them, what they did for fun and how they managed during the severe winter of 1879. And how they knew what was going on.

The Newspapers

News is always a hot topic, but even more so in the old mining districts where rumors of new strikes and rich veins bathed the rugged camps in a perpetual rosy glow. News circulated by signboard, by word of mouth and through the newspapers. Itinerant editor-publishers, their small presses and cases of handset type with them, wandered from one district to another, to wherever they thought they could make a go of it, following the booms and leaving the busts. They were a witty, crusty, irreverent, perceptive lot. Chronically short of money, they frequently raised cash by offering a part interest in their paper. Their humor ran to wild exaggeration—and their readers recognized it as such. Evidently Houle and Elliott, the publishers of the Bodie *Morning News* felt that Lake District had a future, for they started its first newspaper, the weekly *Lake Mining Review*. For the first few months they printed it in Bodie. The first issue, costing twenty-five cents and delivered by carrier, appeared on 29 May 1879.

Just a month later, William W. Barnes, bringing with him the press he had used to publish the Columbus (Nevada) *Borax Miner* and Benton's *Mono Messenger,* started the semi-weekly *Mammoth City Herald.* Barnes announced that the *Herald* would devote itself to the local news of Bodie, Mammoth City, Mineral Park, Mill City, Pine City and Inyo County, and would include as well any important news from other mining camps, the nation and the world via telegraph. (Mammoth City had no telegraph. I have not yet figured out where the nearest telegraph office might have been—Carson City? Bodie?) Barnes issued its first four-page edition July 2. Subscription rates in October 1879 were $8 a year, $2 for three months or twenty-five cents a copy. By November, 1880, the rates had changed to $5 a year delivered by mail, and fifty cents a month delivered by carrier.

Barnes offered R. D. Bogart, a former editor of the *Virginia Evening Chronicle,* the opportunity to purchase a half-interest in the *Herald.* Bogart agreed and made a down payment of $100 "after a long delay." When Barnes demanded payment of the balance due, Bogart evaded paying by one pretext or another and finally refused

Mastheads of Mammoth City and nearby camps' newspapers.

to pay at all. The rival *Review* observed that although both were competent newspapermen, their being managers together was as unlikely as their being angels in heaven. Apparently Bogart thought he could maneuver Barnes out of control since, in theory, he owned half of the business. Barnes objected and kept demanding payment. Bogart then sued Barnes. When a jury of Lake District citizens decided against Bogart, he "withdrew the suits at his own cost and accepted a compromise."

Apparently the good feelings between Barnes and the lawyer who defended him, Mr. Tubbs, did not last, for several years later the *Bodie Weekly Standard-News* reported that the two had an argument and that Barnes shot Mr. Tubbs. The wounds were superficial.

> Mr. Tubbs states that he had at one time acted as attorney for Barnes in a foreclosure suit against the *Mammoth City Times,* Barnes acting as agent for Marder, Luce & Co., type founders of San Francisco. By the sale of this material to the Bishop Creek *Times* Tubbs had realized nothing on this transaction, including his attorney fee, and he had written to Marder, Luce & Co. about it, asking for his fee.... (1 Feb. 1882)

Bogart, retiring to lick his wounds after his defeat, approached Fred Farnham, an old and bitter enemy of Barnes. Bogart asked Farnham to advance him $600 to purchase the *Lake Mining Review* from Hoole and Elliott. After Farnham moved to Mammoth City, he and Bogart renamed the *Review* and in October began publishing the *Mammoth City Times* as a semi-weekly. Its subscription rates for mail delivery were $8 a year and $3 a month; for delivery by carrier "in vicinity," 25 cents a week.

Both the *Herald* and *Times* were published on Wednesday and Saturday. For several issues the sharpshooting between the two papers was lively and colorful. Bogart ridiculed Barnes and the *Herald,* made puns, accused them of various small crimes and called the *Herald* that "wretched little concern down the street."

> They say that the little *Herald* has virtually passed into the hands of Mr. Tubbs, the lawyer. The little *Herald* ought now to stand on its own bottom.
>
> Private advices from San Francisco reach us to the effect that there are to be assessments on three of our mines within a week or

two. Wonder which they will be: And we wonder if Barnes will steal the official notices from the *Times'* columns, like he did that of the Monte Cristo. *(Times* 22 Oct. 1879)

Barnes fired back in his next issue. To the first accusation, that Tubbs was now controlling the *Herald,* he replied: "If such is the case, the last glimmer of hope is gone for the *Review-Times* to absorb the *Herald.* Got your fingers burnt once on that racket." And replying to the second accusation, he referred back to Mr. Tubbs:

Pshaw, Bogy, stealing a few notices ain't no great crime. Why, bless me, my little man, you tried to get away with the whole of the *Herald* office—but the "bottom" fell out and you had no "tubbs" handy to pack it in before you were caught in the act. *(Herald* 25 Oct. 1879)

Following a particularly vitriolic attack, the *Herald* gave the *Times* a knockout punch in its November first edition, telling it like it was and hitting where it hurt:

"The *Times* is the only newspaper published in Mammoth." [A claim made by Bogart that was obviously not true.] Yes, the only "newspaper" whose editor is an avowed bribe taker, and whose columns are filled with misrepresentations of the camp that gives him support.

In December John Gilson purchased the *Times* and Bogy was relegated to editor. However, by January 1880 Bogy's interest in Lake District seemed to have cooled considerably; Hugh Glenn from Aurora, Nevada, and B. H. Yaney took over the *Times.* George Forbes speculated that Farnham and Bogart were forced out for failing to submit their articles to the Mammoth Mining Company for review and approval. While some evidence lends credence to this charge, other reports suggest that Bogart's debts had caught up with him.

Once the new owner took over, the *Times* became a well-run newspaper, fully matching the *Herald* in local news coverage. Both papers relied on ads and business cards (classified ads that looked like business cards) to cover most of their operating expenses. One page of the 22 October 1879 *Herald* contained thirty-eight ads and business cards. Among the professional men advertising with cards were two doctors, five attorneys, a constable, a U.S. Deputy Mineral Surveyor, a mining recorder, a surveyor-civil engineer and an assayer.

Among the businesses advertising were a sawmill, three livery/feed stables, two breweries, two general merchandise stores, five hotels or lodging houses, two restaurants, five saloons, a drug store, two cigar stores, a stationer's store and the two newspapers. The content of the ads ranged from a simple statement that one was in business at a given location to a listing of inventory, a format used repeatedly by George Rowan for his general store. The Pacific Restaurant run by 48-year-old Mary Winter from England and 28-year-old Kate Lester from Wisconsin advertised in bold type "none but white cooks employed by us." Given its small population and limited number of advertisers, it is a wonder that for a time Lake District sported two newspapers.

Bill Chalfant, 1868–1943

Because I will be quoting extensively from W. A. (Willie Arthur) Chalfant in the pages that follow, perhaps this is the best place to explain that he too was an eastern Sierra newspaperman. His father, Pleasant A. (P. A.) Chalfant, and James A. Parker (who discovered the Alpha claim, as mentioned in chapter two) started the first newspaper in Owens Valley, the *Inyo Independent,* in 1870. P. A. eventually moved from Independence to Bishop, where in 1885 he founded the *Inyo Register.* Bill ran the newspaper for him with the help of B. H. Yaney (mentioned above as part-owner of the *Mammoth City Times*) until 1889, when he became sole owner; he remained as publisher and editor until 1942. His books and columns are among the most important sources of eastern Sierra history. Chalfant interviewed and corresponded with most of Owens Valley's pioneers, and he gleaned information from numerous sources, such as old newspapers, official reports and documents, and manuscripts in the library of Henry G. Hanks (an assayer in Owens Valley mining camps in 1863, and later State Mineralogist of California, whose library burned in the San Francisco fire of 1906). Undoubtedly his stories of the Mammoth mine came firsthand from Parker and Yaney and others who had worked in Lake District.

...y of the proceedings of
The meeting then ad-
meet at the same place on
ing, December 26th, when
committees will be expected
ports.

lipse of the Sun.

be an eclipse of the sun Jan-
e eclipse will be invisilbe
drawn through St. Joseph,
l Baton Rouge, Louisiana.
e western quarter of North
Pacific ocean and extreme
e of Austalia—being central
ong a line distant twenty
f and parallel to a line drawn
terey, California, Mariposa,
ke City. Elsewhere it will
The eclipse will begin as fol-
er, Colorado, 4h. 1m. P. M;
New Mexico, 4h. 1m. P. M;
y, Utah, 3h. 24m. P. M; Vic-
uver Island, 2h. 25m. P. M;
egon, 2h. 29m. P. M; San
. 35m. P. M; Monterey, Cal-
8m. P. M; Sacramento City,
; Stockton, 2h. 40m. P. M;
. 47m. P. M; San Diego, 3h.
irginia City, 2h. 48m. P. M;
ng more or less eclipsed. At
tralia, the sun will rise on
of January 12 slightly eclips-
e contuing for fifteen min-
year there will be six eclipses
d two of the moon.

M. C. Joint Tunnel.

lement weather has had no
workings, which have been
ied forward. They have now
ely through the conglomer-
n in which they have been
d are now in solid rock.
aking on an average about
r day. Should this rate of
tinue they will, according to
e the ledge by the opening

eer Ball To-Night.

guiding hand of Mr. J. L.
d by the good taste of Mrs.
Miss Lizzie Ratter, Giles'
n most beautifully decorated
ens, pictures and flags, for
Ball to night, and when we
upper is to be gotten up by
f connoisseurs, Al. Currier,
ow that everything will be
e. The beauty and chivalry
be there.

LOST.

Lumber Delivered,
when desired, to any part of Mammoth, Mill,
or Pine City.
MAMMOTH STEAM SAWMILL CO.
au6-tt

LAKE AND BODIE STAGE LINE.

**Carrying U. S. Mails and Wells, Far-
go & Co.'s Express.**

STAGES LEAVE MAMMOTH CITY FOR
KING'S RANCH and BODIE every morning at four o'clock.

TIME TO BODIE, TWELVE HOURS,

Where close connection is made with the Carson Stage Line.

Fare to Bodie...........Fifteen Dollars

Returning, Stages leave BODIE on the arrival
of the U. S. Mail from CARSON, arriving in
MAMMOTH CITY at nine o'clock, P. M.

OFFICE—At Standard Hotel, Mammoth Ave-
hne. WM. BLACKMORE, Proprietor.
ROBT. TRIGG, Agent o18-tf
J. R. SIMON. H. G. SIMON

J. R. SIMON & CO.,

Wholesale and Retail Dealers in

GENERAL MERCHANDISE,

GROCERIES, PROVISIONS,

HARDWARE, STEEL, IRON,

CLOTHING, BOOTS & SHOES,

TOURISTS' OUTFITS, MINERS' OUTFITS,

DRY GOODS and FANCY GOODS

A SPECIALTY.

Orders promptly attended to. Goods delivered free of charge.
J. R. SIMON & CO.
-tf Main street, Mammoth City.

A CARD.

To the Citizens of Lake District and the Traveling Public.

I WISH TO ANNOUNCE THAT A CHANGE
of proprietorship in the Lake District and
Round Valley Toll Road has been made. Hav
ing bought the interest of Mr. J. W. Davis, I
intend now to give all my personal attention to
the road, which shall be kept in good repair;
and I will guarantee fair dealing with all par-
ties. I shall also reduce the rates of local travel.
Thanking the pub ic generally for the past good
feeling toward my brother and myself, I promise faithfully to study the interest of all, and try
in every respect to give entire satisfaction to one
and all, and hope to receive kind and fair treat-
ment from the citizens of Mammoth and surrounding country. I am respectfully yours,
J. W. DICKINSON.
Mammoth City, Nov 22, 1879. n23-tf

---

shoes and Newport Ties.

MEN'S AND BOYS' HATS AND CAPS.

Wool Hats and Beaver Hats, of all sizes, colors and grades.

PLENTY TO SATISFY HUNGER, SUCH AS

GROCERIES AND PROVISIONS.

Canned Fruits, Meats	Coal Oil,
and Vegetables,	Dried Fruits,
Catsups, Pickles,	Crackers,
Pepper Sauce,	Ham, Bacon, Lard,
Worcestershire Sauce,	Butter, Cheese,
Coffee, Tea,	Flour, Corn Meal,
Sugar, Syrup,	Graham, Oat Meal,
Mackerel,	Hominy, Potatoes.
Candles,	Flavoring Extracts.
Soap,	Spices, Candies, Etc.

TOBACCO, CIGARS, CIGARITAS, ETC.

MINERS' TOOLS, AND A FULL LINE OF

HARDWARE.

Picks, Shovels,	Hat Hooks,
Axes, Saws,	Can Openers,
Hatchets, Hammers,	Cork-screws,
Braces and Bits,	Butcher Knives,
Screw-drivers,	Carving Knives,
Door Bolts,	Skinning Knives,
Strap Hinges,	Table Knives & Forks,
Door Locks and Bolts,	Table Spoons,
Padlocks,	Tea Spoons,
Hasps and Staples,	Tacks, Nails, Bolts,
Screws, Screw Hooks,	Nuts and Washers,

I MAKE A SPECIALTY IN THE SELECTION
of quality and variety of my

TINWARE.

Galvanized Iron Buck-	Custard Pans,
ets, Tin Buckets,	Jelly Plates, Pie Plates,
Lunch Buckets,	Tin Plates,
Tin Camp Kettles,	Cups, Dippers,
Russia Iron Camp Ket-	Oil Cans, Zinc Oilers.
tles, Sauce Pans,	Wagon Oilers,
Fry Pans, Bread Pans,	Egg Beaters,
Dish Pans, Milk Pans,	Nutmeg Graters.

BUYERS WILL FIND WITHOUT EQUAL
in this section, my stock of

QUEENSWARE AND GLASSWARE.

Sauce Tureens,	Wine Goblets,
Cups and Saucers,	Beer Mugs,
Plates, Tea Pots,	Bar Glasses,
Butter Bowls,	Fruit Dishes,
Sugar Bowls,	Cake Dishes,
Water Pitchers,	Pickle Dishes,
Milk Pitchers,	Salt Dishes,
Beer Pitchers,	Glass Setts.
Bowls and Pitchers,	Water & Milk Pitchers,
Soap Slabs,	China Cups & Saucers,
Side Dishes,	Mugs, Toy Setts,
Sauce Dishes, Platters,	Candlesticks, Vases,
Water Goblets,	Lamps and Lanterns.

A WELL SELECTED STOCK OF

DRUGS AND MEDICINES.

Patent Medicines, Hair Tonic, Hair Vigor.
Cough Medicines, Pills, Oils, Salts,
Bitters, Troches, Camphor,
Hamburg Tea, Etc., Etc.

ALSO, LOCAL AGENT FOR THE SALE OF
the

FLORENCE, WHITE AND WEED

SEWING MACHINES.
All of which I will sell at the lowest living
rates, FOR CASH, or take produce in exchange.
1-tf GEO. W. ROWAN

Mammoth City Herald, 24 December 1879.

Food, Goods, Wages and Prices

The local stores and the goods they had in stock were always a subject of keen interest and much comment. Both the *Times,* in its column "About Town," and the *Herald,* in its column titled "Tailings," kept track of shipments as they arrived. For example:

> Received this week: a consignment of general merchandise and winter stock for P. A. Wagner & Co. on lower Mammoth Ave.

> Rice & Hause's mail sleigh, drawn by two horses en tandem, arrived Monday at 2 P.M. with the mail from Bodie, reporting the road in good sleighing condition. (*Herald* 19 Nov. 1879)

Many of the stores, in turn, advertised their wares in both papers. George Rowan, owner of the largest general store, offered an amazing variety of goods. Among the groceries he advertised were cheese, dried fruits, crackers, coffee, tea, sugar, flour, corn meal, oat meal, graham flour, beef, mutton and lard. Hardware advertised included such items as miners' tools, butcher knives, door butts, stoves, Vulcan Blasting Powder and fuse. Tinware included tin plates, custard pans, lunch buckets, dippers, nutmeg graters and wagon oilers.

Fresh food was often in short supply; when available, it brought high prices. In winter it became even more expensive. The 23 November 1879 *Herald* reported that eggs were "selling at five bits [$62^1/_2$ cents] a dozen." Two months later they cost almost twice as much. The *Times* noted that eggs had arrived on January 13 and that "the party who had them only asked $8^1/_2$ cents apiece for them" (21 January 1880). A previous edition reported that some merchants were storing beef in large quantities to supply the town through the winter. Potatoes were very scarce; Jim Sherwin reportedly carried in eighty pounds on his back and sold them for a dollar a pound.

Franklin Buck, in the spring of 1879, observed happily that Lake District was enjoying cosmopolitan delights from San Francisco:

> From Mammoth we can go to Mojave Station on the Southern Pacific R.R. by way of Owens Lake, 140 miles, and then to San Francisco by R.R. There is a steamboat on Owens Lake. It takes two days and costs 25 dollars to get to San Francisco. We are supplied

with fresh fish, salmon, etc., and strawberries and green peas, etc., from Sacramento and San Francisco, now, at high prices, but we have everything to eat and drink here at reasonable prices for a new country. Splendid food at 50 cts a meal and 8 dollars a week. (30 April 1879)

Buck, writing to his relatives, may have been overstating the abundance of fresh food. The following detailed account from the *Herald* is probably more candid about food supplies and their prices. Quoted here at length, it covers many facets of the market and reveals that the new district's growth clearly was straining the food supply.

Our markets are generally well supplied with fresh meats, and are likely to be so long as there are cattle feeding upon a thousand hills. In the matter of beef, mutton, pork, veal, etc., our prices vary but little from retail figures in San Francisco, and if a purchaser knows his business, he can find just as good a quality. Chickens are scarce and rather high, but eggs from Round and Long Valleys find their way to town about twice a week, and are retailed from wagons at 35 and 40 cents a dozen. Eastern eggs are also obtainable, but one needs to be a little critical in the selection of them—some have been a long time out of the memory of the hens that laid them. In the matter of cured provisions, the various stores are well supplied. Hams (Eastern) rate at about 25 cents a pound, and bacon at 18 and 20. Groceries are about fifteen per cent higher than retail prices at the Bay [San Francisco], but the articles supplied are of first grade. Milk is supplied by a rancher at the foot of the grade at $12^{1}/_{2}$ cents a quart; but for butter we are mostly dependent on the outside world. This butter comes in barrels, and some of it—but we forbear. The Round Valley farmers bring in a little butter, but it is nearly always poorly made and anything but attractive to the eye. Besides, it frequently is so ill-fitted for a forty-mile journey that its offense becomes rank and smells to heaven. We are worse off for vegetables than anything else. Potatoes about as big as walnuts bring five and six cents a pound, and other vegetables are poor, scarce and very dear. We are now mostly dependent on canned goods, but it is hoped that when the Valley ranchers wake up to the fact that we have a market here for their products, they will rustle around and make the earth more fruitful of things we need. Hay and grain are high—so high, indeed, that the average horse eats off his head in just two months. Hay—wire grass hay at that—sells for $45 a ton, and barley brings about 4 cents a pound.... Fruit is scrumpy, small and not over toothsome. Peaches, nectarines, grapes and apples are the chief varieties.... To simplify accounts the fruit wagons sell all as it comes for 12$^1/_2$ cents a pound, until crow's feet are seen, and the silent worm that gnaws introduces himself, when with a true spirit of enterprise, competition and want-to-get-home-ativeness the sagacious dealer subjects the remainder of his stock to a shameful sacrifice, and sells it at 10 cents. The chief luxury we have...are trout.... These are caught by the Indians in the South Fork of the San Joaquin, and retailed at about 50 cents a dozen. (13 August 1879)

This last sentence is particularly interesting, as it reflects the absence of native trout in most eastern Sierra lakes and streams. Although many waters now teem with trout, all have been planted. As early as 1879 the *Herald* suggested that the State Fish Commission stock Mammoth's lakes. Apparently they, or a private party, heeded the *Herald*'s suggestion, for just a few years later Old Charley caught trout in Lake Mary for the picnic Helen Doyle described. The stream the *Herald* calls the South Fork, known today as Fish Creek, is *west* of the Sierra crest.

Unlike groceries which were often in short supply and expensive, whisky was abundant and cheap and frequently mentioned by the papers. In an article titled "Off the Track," the 13 September 1879 *Herald* commented that there was "no tanglefoot in town" and that the saloons were selling only Miner's Joy and Woodchopper's Delight, both whiskies of local manufacture. The same issue also noted that, on the whole, sales were not good due to the nature of Mammoth City's "over-temperate citizens." (We can only wonder if that comment is tongue-in-cheek or the Mammoth Mining Company's attempt to burnish Mammoth City's image.) On August 13 the *Herald* noted that "[m]ost of the saloons in town have reduced their prices to one bit [one-eighth of a dollar]." Did this indicate a generous supply on hand or, rather, that the district's imbibers just did not care much for the homemade product that, at best, was raw, potent and thirty days old? The Temple of Folly, a saloon that ran frequent ads, in November advertised a new drink:

Mammoth City Herald, 15 November 1879.

Rock & Rye at the Temple of Folly. The new remedy for coughs, colds, etc. Everybody drinks it. *(Mammoth City Times* 12 Nov. 1879)

Advertised prices for a cord of wood in October were "$4 on the ground and $5 delivered." Each dwelling stored quantities of wood for the winter. It was cut near Pine City and sledded to Mammoth City after the first snow.

To appreciate what these prices meant to a Mammoth City miner, let us relate them to what he earned, probably three dollars a day and certainly no more than four. That is three dollars a *day*, not an *hour;* for a ten- or twelve-hour day, six days a week. If he bought his meals at the Yosemite Chop House at 50¢ a meal or $8 a week, that meant almost half a week's pay went for meals. If he ate at Anderson's Restaurant on Mammoth Avenue, he paid 40¢ a meal, one dollar for a 3-meal ticket or $7 for a 21-meal ticket. Or, if he cooked his own food, the *Herald's* prices quoted above give an idea of costs to feed a family.

Cash Problems

Many advertisers expressly stipulated that their goods were available only for cash. For emphasis their ads often stated "This is no humbug!" or "Call and be convinced of the fact" or "Wares and merchandise for cash—and no foolishness."

The cash problem is partly explained in Tom Rigg's letter to Adele Reed: "Everything was stock then, you paid for laundry, meals and so on, with stock" (1982). Mark Twain described a similar situation during Virginia City's flush times. "Every man had his pockets full of stock, and it was the actual custom of the country to part with small quantities of it to friends without the asking" (1872). George Forbes described the shortage of cash in more detail, although he spoke of checks rather than stock; today we would call it scrip.

> The trouble is, there is no money...currency is something... unknown.... All the companies pay in checks on San Francisco, and, by so doing, save two per cent—the cost of bringing up gold. Many of the merchants, or, should I say all, are obliged to keep some small change on hand, which is reluctantly doled forth when you cannot be induced to take anything more from their

— Messrs. Lawler & Harrigan, ontgomery street, are sole agents francisco for the MAMMOTH MES.

RAVELER'S GUIDE.

Bodie Stage Line.
Mammoth City for Bodie daily at odie for Mammoth daily on the ar- Carson stages.

rivals and Departures.
s.—Jas. Morgau, Mr. Parke, Wm. , L. A. Scowden, A. Y. Ross, J. R. . Higgins.
rss—P. H. Ward, D. Mahoney, and, G. P. McLeod, Hector Forbes, ox, M. P. Wolff, L. J. Moyse, Jas. r. Parke, L. A. Scowden, A. Y.

Notice.
. M. Maddox, formerly with Kopp, will hereafter collect scriptions for the MAMMOTH ies. Subscribers will please mpt payment every Monday

ABOUT TOWN.

Enright & Mayne's for your hats.

stimated that 2,000 cords of ve been piled up in town dur- ast week.

gain have an abundance of ur streets. Oh, for a gale to around.

Reardon is getting along as ould be expected, and will no about town in due time.

ountain fever is in town, e the health of all Mam- is splendid.

rue Blue boarding house at h of the tunnel is completed pied by the men.

has been an improvement in h stock. The last reported e 200 shares at 7.

norning there was a leaden in the heavens, which be- e approach of a storm.

urphy has moved into the formerly occupied by Rein- olf, where he will open a

A MINING COMPLICATION.

THE HEADLIGHT COMPANY IN A SNARL.

THE MINE JUMPED BY MORRIS BURKE AND OTHERS.

What the Row is All About.

Mining circles in Mammoth have been somewhat agitated for a day or two over certain complications on top of the hill, affecting the Headlight Mining Co. The other morning Morris Burke and N. D. Smith went up to the mine, and quietly clapped on notice of a new location, put up their stakes and entered into formal posses- sion. The same day ex Senator Stew- art and James Morgan arrived in town, and it was soon whis- pered about that Burke's re-loca- tion and their coming had more or less connection. Subsequent develop- ments showed that they had, but not exactly in the way the public im- agined. It seems that the complica- tion is brought to a focus by the in- terruption to the granting of a patent for the Headlight Company, some account of which, with the reasons, was published in the last issue of the TIMES. As is known, the Headlight patent is being opposed by persons owning a claim called the Vivian, which is now said to have passed into the hands of Morgan and others. The Vivian people claim that 625 feet of the ground for which the Headlight is now seeking a patent, belongs to them by priority of location; that when the Mammoth ground came to be surveyed for a patent, it was found that to make up the 1,500 feet re- quired it would be necessary to float the south end over about 700 or 800 feet of Headlight ground. The Head- light consented to this, gave a deed and then to recoup itself moved its own line south an equal number of feet. But in doing this it is claimed it took in the Vivian 625 feet, and that is why the latter has made such a per- sistent fight against the patent. Some time ago, it is said, Morgan, the Vivian claimant, sent up to Morris Burke, Mining Recorder of Lake dis- trict, for an abstract of the records relating to all these complications, and Burke made the abstract, and charged

The Air Compressor and Boilers in Place, and the Work Almost Ready to Begin—A Feeble Protest From San Francisco.

A short trip up to the Monte Cristo- Headlight tunnel site shows with what tremendous energy Superintendent Hardy, acting for both companies, has prosecuted the work of prepara- tion. Operations began barely three weeks ago, and already a large build- ing has been constructed for the air compressor and boilers, foundations built and the machinery all put in place. In addition a large boarding house has been built, a coal house erected, and two or three hundred cords of wood cut, hauled and piled. Mr. Hardy says that in a week at furthest he would have been ready to start the drills. This morning, how- ever, he was served with a formal notice from the officers of the Lake View Company, in San Francisco, pro- testing against the occupancy of their ground by the tunnel buildings, but as the buildings are already there we don't believe they will be removed. A few "scads," judiciously applied in San Francisco, will no doubt soon heal the outraged feelings of the Lake Viewers. At any rate we feel quite well assured that the matter will soon be adjusted in some way. The occu- pancy of the Lake View ground was probably the result of some misunder- standing. When President Thomp- son of the Monte Cristo Company was here making arrangements to start the work, it was understood that he had permission to put the site on Lake View ground, but it seems he must have been mistaken. It only remains now for the companies to either re- move their buildings or do what they ought to have done in the first place— make equitable arrangements with the Lake View, and put the thing in black and white. Business is busi- ness always.

LOCAL MINING NOTES.

C. C. Radcliffe is expected in to-night with 50 pounds of rock from the South End mines.

Mergenthaler & Harst's Columbia mine, at the South End, is said to be looking well—in fact better than ever.

The Don Quixote tunnel is in 185 feet; ground hard and difficult to work.

A legal squabble is threatened be- tween the Metallic Con. and the Ophir, but it will probably be fixed up in a day or two.

Superintendent Hardy is now

Mammoth City Times, 1 November 1879.

shelves. This change is of the cheapest kind—any coin which sells below par in San Francisco—such as English shillings (given for a quarter), Mexican and Chilean dollars (at 100 cents), five franc pieces (the same value) and all the coins of the Continent of Europe which can by any stretch of imagination, be assimilated to round values—parts into which a quarter of a dollar will divide evenly. If they ever descend to small change I look forward confidently to the circulation of Chinese cash, which will be passed over the counters at the nominal rate of a dime each.

I very much doubt if any of Mammoth's merchants ever saw small change in use—any coin less than a quarter. A ten-cent piece is of no value—will not purchase even a darning needle. If I require some small article which elsewhere retails at one to two cents, I am asked two bits for it with an air which is impressive as showing that the shopkeeper believes that he is doing me an immense favor in keeping and handling or selling any such petty article. Thus he keeps on piling up the quarters—always the quarter in his favor—even adding the small coin to the sixty-dollar bill which I have just purchased as the result of my after-thought on the matter of a three-cent gimblet. Even with very limited transactions this course must tell favorably on the right side of the profit and loss account, but after all is a poor offset to a mean and demoralized man. (14 Jan. 1880)

School and Library

For those whose interests went beyond newspaper feuds and merchandise ads, there were many activities to choose from. Although there was no school building, classes for all ages were conducted by "Miss Fleming" in a borrowed room in the Magnolia Hall on Mammoth Avenue. According to the 31 July 1880 *Herald*, the evening of August 6 was set aside for a benefit ball to raise money for a school building. Subsequent hard times forestalled actual work on the project. For those who considered themselves too old for the scholastic devotions of Miss Fleming, A. J. Murphy offered his personal library to the community. An educated man who had studied for the priesthood, Murphy housed his circulating library in his popular saloon, The Temple of Folly. (A Temple of Folly photograph, frequently displayed in Mammoth Lakes and mistakenly identified as Mammoth City, is—alas—Main Street in Bishop.)

Music and Drama

Despite long hours of hard physical work, life in Lake District was not unrelieved drudgery. The miners worked hard but they also played hard. Fun-filled diversions were many and varied.

Singing and dancing lessons were available in Hutchinson Hall (what a long way these miners have come since the gold camps of 1850!) And, according to the 31 August 1879 *Herald,* there were two bands: The Silver Star Band and The Amateur Mozarts, "a local organization of musicians and good fellows" whose performances commanded $1.50 for a reserved seat. There was also the Mammoth City Dramatic Club. On 7 February 1880, it presented a benefit for William Haines in which *Miralda* and *The Rough Diamond* played to a packed house. (Haines's feet and hands had been frozen while he tried to bring in the mail.) A few months later *The People's Lawyer* and *Good for Nothing* played at the Magnolia Opera House, followed by *The Silver Star Band* which demonstrated its talents at a dance held for "all comers."

A marriage was a major, but infrequent, event; by early 1880 the papers had reported only two of them. The one on Valentine's Day stirred warm feelings throughout the camp and the *Herald* expressed the fond wishes of all. "May happiness attend them, and as they drift along the rough ledges of life, may they encounter nothing but pay rock" (18 Feb. 1880). With only occasional lapses into violence and lawlessness, this socially conscious community actively supported many meetings, dances, lectures, benefits, picnics and cultural presentations.

Fishing and Hunting

The changing of the seasons brought different sports and pleasures. During the fall, while Lake District basked in Indian summer, the *Times* reported ducks and the promise of good hunting on Casa Diablo Lake a few miles to the northeast. The "ducks found there are grey mallard, sprig tail and a smaller variety that resemble teal, but are of a different plumage (22 November 1879)." Fishing, too, was popular, although it involved riding some distance—over the crest to the Sierra's western slope where fish were plentiful. Franklin Buck, describing such a fishing trip on 23 July 1880, commented on the country as well as their good luck:

> Last week I went fishing over the summit on the South Fork of the San Joaquin, about 12 miles, Forbes [John P. Forbes, age 40 from Nova Scotia, one of the company's superintendents], Major R. and an Indian, Jim.... We found regular down East brakes [rough land heavily overgrown], strawberries, alder swamps, rattle snakes, deer, quail and plenty of trout. We camped right by a soda spring, just like soda out of a fountain...but we had no syrup to go with it.
>
> The scenery is equal to Yosemite. About two miles below our camp we found a Chinaman with 2000 sheep. The night before a California lion got amongst them and killed eight. We found a fat lamb not dead and had lamb chops added to our bill of fare. We had a fine time and stayed four days.

Casa Diablo Hot Springs

Buck described another favorite spot, the hot springs, in a letter from Mammoth City dated 29 June 1879:

> Then I went down to the Hot Springs, five miles below town. At the springs the water boils. Will cook potatoes in 17 minutes. It is as large as six feet in diameter and boils up two feet below. There is a nice bath house where I bathed. Could just bear it. The water contains sulphur and iron and is quite a resort for people who want a clean wash.

National Politics

During 1880, the national election stirred up considerable excitement. The Democrats' platform generally appealed more to western miners than did the Republicans'. The Democratic platform included a provision that gold, silver and paper money could readily be converted into each other *(cheap money,* in contrast to using only gold coins). It also favored an amendment to the Burlingame Treaty that would have stopped all Chinese immigration "except for travel, education and foreign commerce and therein carefully guarded" *(Mammoth City Herald* 6 Nov. 1880). Western mining camps, with their sometimes bitter and always outspoken anti-Chinese prejudice, strongly supported this amendment. Consequently, Lake District s, is still sloshing around town enjoying the fine weather of this altitudinous town.

It is reported that J. D. Collins, the carpenter, who went from here to Bodie a short time since, is down with pneumonia at that place and not expected to recover.

Mr. Tubbs' handsome little cottage on Mammoth avenue is almost completed. The front has received its first coat of paint and presents quite a handsome appearance.

Fred Farnham's shed in an obscure alley-way in the rear of Gillson & Barber's store, and adjoining Bogart's little white cabin, was hastily thrown together in a couple of days last week.

Would it not prove advantageous to owners of property at the South End if they would amongst themselves give some decisive names to the eight lakes in that vicinity.

Jim Logan returned from a prospecting trip south of Lake a couple of days ago. Jim says it's the devil's own country down through there, and uncomfortably full of bears.

Mr. A. J. Murphy will open a first-class saloon in the building lately occupied by Reinstein & Wolf. Mr. Murphy intends to make this a pleasant resort for his many friends this winter.

Mr. Mell, the stone mason, has discovered a bed of clay in close proximity to Mammoth which he thinks will make good brick, and he proposes to give it a trial in the Spring by burning a few hundred thousand.

Billy Blackmore's Nevada saloon is made to resound nightly with a concord of sweet sounds from Bob Young's old Cremona. Bob is a master hand with the violin, and can produce just such harmony as pleases all lovers of good music.

The citizens of Mammoth generally are laying in a large supply of Winter wood, and those who have neglected to do so will have no trouble in "nipping" enough o' dark nights. The Review-Times hasn't a stick in sight, though the nights and mornings are rather sharp and frosty.

Now that we have a daily mail it is rather uncertain. The postoffice officials at Bodie amuse themselves occasionally by sending the Mammoth mail to Bridgeport and the Bridgeport mail to us. The newspapers of that suicidal burg have drove the Postmaster nearly crazy, and he has forgotten the points of the com-

in the world. For of such is the kingdom of heaven.

Deserves Success.

Al Currier and Miss Lizzie Rutter evidently know how to cater to the public taste, as their increased business has rendered it necessary to enlarge their dining-room. The large room formerly used as a saloon is being tastefully fitted up, and when completed Al can accommodate all the hungry that apply. The dining-room will be presided over by Miss Rutter and Mrs. Currier, whose pleasant and accommodating manners serve to render the savory dishes all the more palatable. Al is a rustler and deserves success.

No More Milk Till Spring.

Our supply of the lacteal secretion has been cut off, and the average baby is disconsolate. So is his sisters, his cousins and his aunts. Mr. Sears, who has been supplying our citizens with a pure, fresh article of milk for some months past, has concluded to winter at his ranch at Big Pine, some ninety miles from here, as the high price of feed would not justify him in running his dairy at this place through the Winter. He left this morning, taking his stock with him, but announces his intention of returning in the Spring.

The Coming Shipment.

Superintendent Hardy informs us that the first clean-up of the new Mammoth mill is now being made, and in a few days the first shipment of bullion will be sent to San Francisco by the company. It is impossible to-day for us to give the exact figures, but will do so in our next issue. Mr. Hardy has sent to Bodie for the shot-gun messengers to guard the treasure to Carson. This is required by Wells, Fargo & Co. as an additional safeguard.

Eating Crow.

After a good cussin' Farnham's little man Bogart has executed another summersault and craw-fishes out of his $5 rock item by saying that his blundering types made him say $5 when he meant $15. Probably if the "only" reliable mining journalist had got a sound drubbing the rock would have been worth $50. But maybe he's right for once—for Bogart would ruin the most truthful font of type in a month.

Rumored Strike.

Rumors have been rife on the streets for the past four days of another rich find in the Mammoth mine—this time in the lower tunnel. Being unable to get any particulars we simply give the rumor for what it is worth.

location on a ledge lying and west of the last named called it Mineral Chief. about twenty feet wide, in During this month Messrs. and Terrence Kelly have mad tions south of the above, sh beautiful orange quartz, wh little depth must prove a va The locations are named Cu terion. They run northwest west. Phil Mackey and J. C also a claim on the same most encouraging one, called and those who know the grit of the owners hope to see up a valuable property.

Other Items.

The owners of the Chris lumbus have taken up a mil end of Lake Massie, also a on Darmet Creek, where th ready turned the water and c short distance, showing a de to win if muscle and perse accomplish it.

Altogether the outlook fo promising discovery is rose-c with an exhibition of pluck the fortunate discoverers can carve a fortune therefrom future.

Going to Bodie.

Mr. Moyse, who has so abl the business of Reinstein & V town during the past Summer up the business of that firm moth, and will take the rem to Bodie, where the firm are a large house in the drygood ing line. Mr. Moyse has i friends during his stay am we bespeak for him a call quarters by visiting Mammo

Not So Bad.

It is rather a hard matte idle man in Mammoth at pr camp is not overrun with m older and larger camps, and t are here find ready employme nerative prices. Considerin ter has set in, this is not so b present pleasant weather is advantage of and all kinds of ing pushed ahead.

The "E. N." Soci

The E. N.'s give their fi Giles' Hall to-morrow evenin fair promises to be a very pl as the gentlemen composin are among our best known c every preparation has been enjoyable time by the lovers sichorean art. Tickets can b drug store of Willis & Ste

Mammoth City Herald, 29 October 1879.

followed the 1880 contest between Republican James Garfield and Democrat Winfield Scott Hancock with enthusiasm. Mammoth voters split their votes evenly, forty-four each for Garfield and Hancock, but Garfield won the national election. Although the *Herald* endorsed Hancock, it reported the campaigns with good humor. The second excerpt below is from an article titled "Jollification."

> An Indian brought in a splendid young eagle.... Jim Wales bought the bird and has him perched in front of the Delta saloon where visitors gaze upon him in distant admiration. Jim has named the bird "young Hancock," but if the election returns don't commence chopping soon he will have to undergo a new baptism.

> A portion of the Republicans of Mammoth started a bonfire, fired anvils and otherwise deported themselves jubilantly after the arrival of the stage last night [bringing news of Garfield's victory]. Can't quite swear that it sounded nice to Democratic ears. (6 Nov. 1880)

Prostitution

When it came to the profession that catered solely to the menfolk, especially on payday, Mammoth City was no different from other mining camps. The presence of seven prostitutes in the 1880 census should not pass without comment. After all, they comprised one percent of the population, and others may have been present but camouflaged behind such classifications as cook or housewife. (A common label for a prostitute in the Kansas cow towns was *waitress.)* Of the seven prostitutes, five were from China, ages 36, 32, 25, 23 and 20; one of them was a wife as well. Sara Smith, age 23, was from Ohio; and Mammoth City's only black resident, Rebecca E. Simmons, age 28, was from Nova Scotia. In the 1880s, most mining camps tolerated and even accepted these women and their activities. Contemporary sources mention them little if at all. It seems that the "good folk" understood, and permitted without fanfare, what the English during this Victorian period had openly acknowledged in Parliamentary discussion: that it was socially preferable for hot-blooded young men to bed down with prostitutes than with the Victorians' own daughters.

Scuffles

While Lake District was relatively free of serious and violent crime, now and then the men indulged in their own sort of fun. As the *Herald* remarked on 13 September 1879:

> There was considerable sport at the Magnolia Saloon. Messrs. Sabin, Mason, Kline and Gallagher tried their skill with each other at a little game of collar and elbow, at which they all showed themselves very proficcient.

Only occasionally did tempers flare to the point of violence; when they did the results could be tragic. The *Herald* reported one such incident:

> A couple of Chinamen quarrled over a gambling game Thursday night, in the basement of an opium den on Main Street, when one pulled his gun and shot the other twice, once in the breast and once in the stomach, killing him instantly. The shootist was arrested soon afterward and lodged in jail where he now lies awaiting examination. (3 Nov. 1879)

The follow-up to this shooting had its amusing aspects and also shows how confused justice in Mammoth City could be.

> The case of Yee See Quan, the Chinaman who was accused of shooting another Chinaman a week or so ago in an opium den, has been before Judge Eddy [the 54-year-old justice of the peace] for several days, on examination. Messrs. Harrison and Tubbs appeared for the prosecution, Messrs. Bequette and Gill for the defense. There was as usual a great conflict of evidence. Poultry is scarce in Mammoth, and therefore the sacredness of the Chinese oaths was somewhat attenuated. Two Chinamen swore they saw Yee See shoot the other Chinaman, while a dozen others swore they didn't. Finally in disgust Judge Eddy dismissed the case. (19 Nov. 1879)

Death in the Camps

Shadows on occasion darkened the robust energy of Lake District; death did not avoid the mining camps. The *Herald*, looking back over the brief history of the district, noted, "Some ten or twelve deaths have occurred: three have been killed in the mines, one burned to death, two lost in the snow" (3 Jan. 1880). Residents located their cemetery well away from the noise and hustle of the town and mill, choosing a location where only the wind disturbed the hallowed silence. Friends and neighbors laid to rest at least seventeen of their fellows during the short time the district flourished.

Time and winter snows took their toll on the cemetery, but vandals have completely destroyed it. I was told that during the 1940s and '50s wooden markers still stood over many of the graves and that many graves still had their original picket or rail fences. I am grieved more deeply than I can express that by 1963 every grave had been vandalized and that the area is now slated for residential development. During a survey conducted for the Forest Service in 1984, I confirmed the age and dimensions of the cemetery, but not the exact number of graves for they are overgrown with brush. I trust you can understand why I prefer not to describe the cemetery's location. Although so much has already been vandalized, I still hope that, despite development plans, what little is left might be allowed to remain in peace.

Winter 1879–1880

We can only wonder whether any of Lake District's residents had the remotest idea of the deep snows and long winters that a 9,000-foot-high Sierra Nevada mining camp is subject to. Even today, with all our snowplows and blowers, heavy snow can isolate Mammoth Lakes for days at a time. The winter of 1879–80 was one of the biggest ever, and Mammoth City, at 8700 feet altitude, was in the direct path of the blizzards that roar over Mammoth Pass.

The storms came late that year but wasted no time in making up for the delay. Snow fell for two days early in December, let up for a few days, and then storms howled continually for eighteen days. According to one resident, twenty-eight feet of snow fell in Lake District that winter. The newspapers reported snow lying eight feet deep on the level.

> Tunnels between business places served for travel within a limited area. Those who came from more distant points, Pine City or one of the other 'cities' along the canyon, or in the neighboring hills, made their way from the top down to the business level on steps

hacked in the snow drifts; as the surfaces became rounded and icy, the incline served as a shute down which incautious pedestrians reached the lower level more expeditiously than intended. (Chalfant 1935)

Wooden stakes marked Mammoth Avenue, according to the *Herald*, and tunnels had to be dug from house to house and from houses to business places. Through it all, Mammoth people looked out for one another. Daily they checked their neighbors' stove pipes sticking above the snow, to make sure that all was well. Smoke signaled a warm fire below, in a dwelling buried under several feet of snow. If no smoke drifted upward, neighbors would call down the stovepipe to make sure that everything was as it should be. Despite the difficulties, people fared reasonably well; merchants had stocked enough food, and good health was the general rule.

During that winter, little mail or news from the outside world reached Mammoth City. William Haines, known around town as "Cleverly" and mentioned above, left on December 20 for King's Ranch to pick up the mail for Mammoth. On the return trip, his mule gave out, overwhelmed by the deep drifts. Haines then took the mail himself and tried to make it on foot. Beginning to tire, he put the mail sack in a tree and, without it, hoped to reach the station at Deadman Summit. Unable to make any headway in the soft snow, in desperation he made camp and lived for two days by a fire he kept going with wood he broke off the lower branches of trees. Realizing that he was beginning to freeze, he tried again to go on to the station, but his "next day's journey was but ten feet" (Chalfant 1942). By the time a search party from Mammoth City reached him, both his hands and his feet were frozen. The rescue party estimated that Haines's mule had given out only half a mile from Deadman station. It took five more days before his rescuers got Haines back to Mammoth City. The whole town set their hearts upon his recovery; but despite the best that 39-year-old Dr. Patrick Ragan could do, including several amputations, Haines died two months later. His mule, rescued by a second party hunting for the mail sack, was taken to a livery stable where it was named Cleverly and eventually nursed back to health.

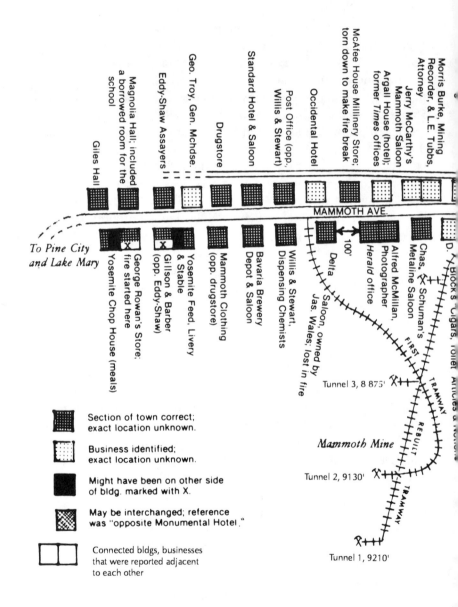

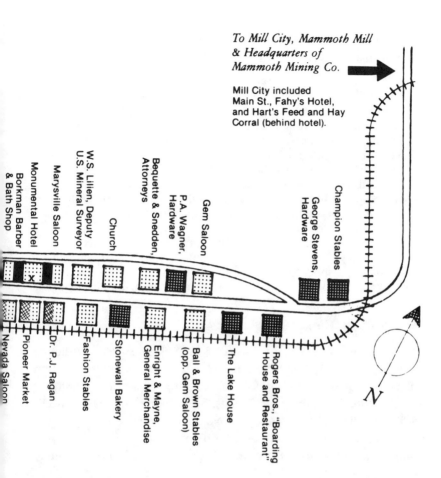

To Mill City, Mammoth Mill & Headquarters of Mammoth Mining Co.

Mill City included Main St., Fahy's Hotel, and Hart's Feed and Hay Corral (behind hotel).

Champion Stables

George Stevens, Hardware

Gem Saloon

P.A. Wagner, Hardware

Bequette & Snedden, Attorneys

Church

W.S. Lilien, Deputy U.S. Mineral Surveyor

Marysville Saloon

Monumental Hotel

Borkman Barber & Bath Shop

Nevada Saloon

Pioneer Market

Dr. P.J. Ragan

Fashion Stables

Stonewall Bakery

Enright & Mayne, General Merchandise

Ball & Brown Stables (opp. Gem Saloon)

The Lake House

Rogers Bros., "Boarding House and Restaurant"

N

MAMMOTH CITY, 1880

Mammoth City 1880 (reconstruction)

Since no plat, original buildings or photographs of Mammoth City have survived, this map is an educated guess, intended to show how the town may have looked. All sites are based on specific references in the *Mammoth City Herald* and the *Mammoth City Times*. The town had several streets, including a Washington Street and a toll road that connected with the upper and lower ends of Mammoth Avenue (originally called Main Street). The two streets shown are based on original sources and on field surveys. (Reconstruction by Gary Caldwell)

When Franklin Buck returned to Mammoth City in July, the winter just endured was a main topic of conversation. As you will discover later in this chapter, what Buck was calling *snow shoes* is not what we call snowshoes at all.

> I went round town talking for two days and listened to all the stories of how deep the snow was, the storms and how this man who we all thought was such a good fellow turned out to be a grand scoundrel and Mrs. So and So lived with a man all winter without any marriage ceremony, house all buried in snow (I don't blame her) and all about Mrs. Bunker having a miscarriage and the Lord only knows what I did hear. It seems they were very much like a lot of passengers on board a vessel who get to hate each other after being shut up together for some time....
>
> The snow fell about 10 feet deep and one storm lasted twenty-three days. They had no mail or communication without going out on snow shoes for four months. They had lots of fun on these snow shoes. It was the only way of getting around. (28 July 1880)

Happy New Year, 1880

The *Times* welcomed the new year of 1880 optimistically, predicting a population of 10,000 for Mammoth City alone, and "the erection of a dozen quartz mills, 110 saloons, banking houses, a new building for the *Times*" (Chalfant 1935). Wishful thinking? Tongue-in-cheek? Stiff upper lip? Wild exaggeration? No doubt all of the above!

According to Chalfant, even in the midst of the winter's severe hardships, Mammoth's people still looked ahead and welcomed holiday festivities:

> Advertising columns of the *Mammoth City Times*...carried announcements of three livery stables, two hotels, five stores, a drug store, a ladies' goods store, five saloons, and other concerns, indicating that Mammoth still had some business hope.
>
> With all the discomforts of the situation, Mammothites were able to find a gayer side. The *Times* observed that "Mammothites believe in enjoying themselves, and they do it. Two parties in a week speak well for their social proclivities." The crowning event was to be an installation ball on New Year's night, given by Mammoth Lodge, No. 50, Knights of Pythias, the only fraternal organization which had secured a foothold. It was to occur in Giles' hall, which had been beautifully decorated for the occasion. (1935)

The ready-made New Year's resolutions offered by the *Herald* in its column titled "Resolves" are a good example of mining camp editors' earthy humor. (Some of the meanings are obscure—your guess is as good as mine.)

Resolved to take your own liquor plain. There is confusion in mixed drinks and bother to the bar-keeper. You may want to stand him off before the year is over, and it is well to cultivate friendly relations.

Keep your vest pockets loaded with two-bit cigars. You thus become an object of interest to your friends.

Don't carry gilt-edge fine-cut [chewing tobacco] for your own use and nigerhead plug for your friends. It is a mean deception.

Eschew the Newport glide, pare down your feet and give the other dancers a chance to live.

When you go to the theater, don't make everybody's life miserable by telling them how much better you saw this thing played in New York or some other seaport.

Don't ask female book-agents to come up to your room and show their books. They are innocent creatures and should not be led into temptation.

Don't gamble in stocks unless you have got a dead point.

Pay a little more attention to your wife and give the hired girl a rest. You won't have so much fun, but it will save you buying hair restorative.

Give your temper the grand bounce. If the other man catches your pedro, omit the usual remarks. (21 Jan. 1880)

Good Times

Despite all the shoveling and tunneling, many folks had enough energy left over to enjoy the snow. Most fun of all was *snow shoeing*. "Last Sunday was a lively day for snow-shoeing, nearly one hundred people being engaged in the sport," reported the *Times* for 21 January 1880. In explaining its popularity, the *Times* had remarked previously that the "delightful uncertainty as to what part will strike the ground first only adds a keener zest to the enjoyment" (13 Dec. 1879). Buck described this pastime, unknown to his Eastern relatives, in a letter dated 28 July 1880. There is no doubt that he was describing what today we call cross-country skiing.

[These snowshoes] are made of a pine plank, 11 feet long and 4 inches wide, turned up at the end like a skate. You scuff along going up hill and going down. You slide, with a long pole to steady you. Men and women get to be very expert on them.

Winter also brought ice on the lakes. The 22 November 1879 issues of both newspapers commented on the prospects of early ice skating. The *Herald* reported "splendid skating on the lakes. The ice is as smooth and as clear as glass." The *Times* lamented that, while skating on Lake Mary was excellent, there were "not more than four or five pairs of skates in town" and these were "in constant use."

However, no one was sorry to see winter's cold, blustery days replaced by the warmer days of summer. Nothing brought more shouts and squeals echoing across the lakes than a July dip into the snow-fed waters. As the *Herald* gleefully observed:

> Bathing in the lower and middle lakes is now all the rage. Last Sunday several persons of both sexes were observed disporting themselves in the pellucid water. It's jolly fun—but the water is still a trifle cold. (30 July 1879)

Of summer's pleasures, the most popular by far were picnics. Throughout the summer, ads for picnics were posted all over town and in both the newspapers. Notices typically ran something like this one: "On Sunday there will be music, dancing, picnicking under the trees, flirting, real love making and we don't know what all" (*Herald* 13 August 1879). The favorite location was Lake Mary, which had sailboats and rowboats for rent at the dock on the eastern shore, a floating barge for dancing and Jerry McCarthy's saloon and dancing pavilion. One *Herald* ad proclaiming "Sail and Row Boats to Let" read:

> Excursion and pleasure parties wishing to enjoy the beautiful scenery of Lake Mary, can be accomodated with row and sail boats upon application to the undersigned, at their wharf on the east side of the lake or to A. B. Anderson at his restaurant on Mammoth Avenue.—MacDonald and McCormic (6 Nov. 1880)

These pleasures were enhanced by a natural lake level lower than today's by six or eight feet. This level provided a greater expanse of lake shore as well as a small island (now drowned) near the western shore. Since it took only a short row to put a couple on this romantic, pine-covered island, picnics there were tremendously

Lake Mary was the favorite place for summer pleasures. According to a *Mammoth City Herald* advertisement, "On Sunday there will be music, dancing, picnicking under the trees, flirting, real love making and we don't know what all" (13 August 1879).

popular. The stories that island could tell! Many a balmy summer evening smiled on Lake Mary as the barge poled out from shore bearing a full complement of band members and dancers, while sailboats and rowboats explored every cove of the lake. The *Herald* (30 July 1879) became truly lyrical describing this idyllic scene:

> Last Sabbath was a most beautiful day, and it was duly taken advantage of by the ladies and gentlemen of Lake District. From an early hour in the morning till long in the night the grand old forest which surround our beautiful lakes resounded with the sound of laughter and song. Gathering wild flowers, singing, love making, lounging under the shade of some huge monarch, sailing and rowing were the order of the day, winding up with a moonlight picnic...we hope to see many such happy days.

Chapter 9

HARD TIMES

The happy new year of 1880 was only a month or two old when the deepening snow brought all operations to a standstill. With the tramway buried and men unable to leave their cabins for days at a time, the mill shut down in March and did not start up again until the first of July.

The onset of winter had already persuaded some miners to head for lower, warmer altitudes; the camp became less and less lively. George Forbes commented on

> the dullness, all pervading deadness, of this mining camp. The storekeepers are sitting reading, idly smoking or lounging against the door casings, vainly looking for a stray customer. Some of the saloons—their name is legion—are empty; in others two or three men sit playing for the drinks in a spiritless kind of way.... There is no bustle on the streets...no wagons loading or unloading, no teamsters shouting and swearing in trying to pass.... (Los Angeles *Evening Express* 14 Jan. 1880)

"Twenty pairs of snowshoes, each with a man on top of them left this morning," lamented the *Mammoth City Times* in its 31 December 1879 edition. And as the snow continued to fall, the papers noted that more and more gold seekers had decided to spend the winter elsewhere:

Above and Opposite. Although this cabin (c. 1860) is not in Lake District, details of its construction illustrate how a cabin was built without finished lumber and with a minimum of nails. A miner often dug his cabin into a slope, for the earth gave warmth and shelter from the fierce winds. Note the notched logs and the hand-hewn shakes.

Men are leaving every day, in twos, sixes, dozens, on snowshoes, barley sacks, anything. A train of wagons and sleds was fully a week making twenty-six miles. In Rock Creek canyon the advance averaged only two miles a day, at incredible cost of labor and much swearing. The livery business has been knocked in the head since Bennett had to sink a double compartment shaft to locate the ridgepole of his stable. (Chalfant 1942)

Franklin Buck Gives Up Mining

The mill's shutdown hastened the emigration considerably, for without a paycheck in sight, the miners' eternal optimism began to waver just a bit. Even Franklin Buck's enthusiasm had cooled. In a May 23 letter from Pioche, Nevada, Buck revealed that, reluctantly, he had decided to give up mining. He was accepting an offer to

take over and gradually buy out the holdings of a long-time friend in the Napa Valley, an area he called "a paradise." It was an offer that was just too good to turn down at age 53.

It will be a humdrum slow business to go picking grapes and milking cows and raising chickens; but, on the other hand, we are getting along in life and we had better take a certainty on having a good living than the uncertainty of making money. If I were years younger I would take the mining camps.

Two months later he wrote from Mammoth City, noting that the mill was now operating and prospects were somewhat brighter. But Buck did not stay; business completed, he left for Napa. A farm was waiting for him.

I got into town about nine o'clock and slept in my own house. I found about the same people I left. The mill and mine are running and although the place is very dull and everybody flat broke and in debt, I think the outlook is better than it was last fall. They have been shut up for four months with snow and the mill only commenced work the 1st of July.

Another letter written the following January from Oakville, 55 miles from San Francisco, expresses the fortunes of so many of the gold seekers. The few hit it rich; the many hit nothing but very hard work and little return. Some continued prospecting all their lives, but most went on to other work. Buck, writing about his farm and how beautiful the land and his life are, says of his mining days:

> I have given it a fair trial and such things are not for me so I am setting out trees and fixing myself comfortably for life right here and I don't know where you can find such a beautiful climate and valley. (22 Jan. 1881)

Something Amiss

Superintendent Hardy left Mammoth City in March, before the mill closed and before news of suspended production reached the newspapers. By themselves, the mill shutting down for the winter and Hardy's departure were not necessarily precursors of difficulties ahead. There were no hints in Mammoth City newspapers that Mr. Hardy would not return or that the mill would not start up again or that the company would not continue to mine. Whether there were local rumors to the contrary we have no way of knowing. When the mill rumbled back into production the first of July, Lake District seemed to be headed for good times again. But at least one man had a premonition that all might not be well. Andrew J. Murphy, proprietor of the Temple of Folly, had painted a large *IF* on the side of a stump near his saloon. If the miners struck some rich veins.... If the mill continued operating.... If the stockholders paid their assessments.... If...if...if....

Although Lake District seemed blissfully ignorant of anything unusual, something was surely amiss. Whatever that something was—we can only guess that the company was going broke—it seemed to be well known in San Francisco. While no negative comments on the Mammoth Mining Company's financial condition were published either in San Francisco or in Lake District, the market's evaluation of the company's future was clearly mirrored in the price of its stock. In the spring of 1879, the stock had risen to $18 and then hit its highest price ever, $20 a share. But as you can see from the following table, in September its price on the San Francisco Stock Exchange began to skid. In December of 1879 company stock fell below $4 a share; within five months it was down to $2 a share. Stockholders saw their investments slide closer and closer to zero.

Opening Prices of Mammoth Mining Company Shares
San Francisco Stock Exchange, August 1879 through November 1880

August 9, 1879	12.50	April 2, 1880	2.50
September 6, 1879	8.50	May 12, 1880	3.25
October 28, 1879	6.50	June 10, 1880	2.50
November 8, 1879	7.00	July 2, 1880	2.00
November 26, 1879	6.00	July 17, 1880	*1.60
December 15, 1879	4.00	September 2, 1880	*1.50
December 18, 1879	2.25	September 16, 1880	1.00
January 3, 1880	*1.70	October 16, 1880	.43
February 5, 1880	3.00	November 1, 1880	.19
March 4, 1880	1.75	November 19, 1880	.06

Starred figures are from the San Francisco Morning Call.
All other figures from the Engineering and Mining Journal.

Assessments Delinquent

Obviously someone knew—perhaps many in San Francisco's financial circles knew—that company finances were in sorry shape. And surely company officers and superintendents knew, for they had been dealing with the problems that had plagued the mill and tramway from the beginning. (Wouldn't it be nice to know how much stock they held and at what point they got rid of it?) The company badly needed money, its expenses continued to outrun its revenue, and its stockholders had been assessed but were not coming forth with their assessments. (Assessing stockholders for a certain amount per share held was a common method of raising more capital. If a company's future was bright, most stockholders would pay their assessment rather than lose their shares. Forfeited shares would be sold at auction with the money going to the company.) Evidently most Mammoth Mining Company stockholders saw little future in their company, for they chose to let their stock go rather than invest more in a mine that had been plagued by questions of poor management and that so far had returned them nothing. On 17 July 1880, the company's assessment on its stockholders fell delinquent. With its stock at a pitifully low $1.60 in July, the company's chance of raising significant capital by selling forfeited stock was nil. In the next four months the stock only dropped lower, finally to six cents a share.

From Dull to Duller

Buck found the camps dull in July; as summer progressed, they became still duller. Early in March 1880 the *Mammoth City Times* had discontinued publication. Little by little even the *Herald* began to wonder whether Mammoth had a future. After confidently predicting in March 1879 that within the next year Lake District would take its place "where she rightfully belongs, in the front rank, with the greatest rich ore and bullion producing districts on the Pacific Coast," in July 1880, in an article titled "Announcement," the *Herald* first gave vent to outright pessimism:

> With this number the *Herald* appears for the first time as a weekly. We have maintained the Wednesday and Saturday editions from the beginning, through all the long Winter, in the hope of a strong revival of business with the coming of warm weather. In this we were in error. It must be acknowledged that Mammoth is dull—very dull. This is no fault of the prospects or developments thus far made, but there seems to be a settled determination to wait until the Mammoth and Headlight and Monte Cristo companies prove the value of the mines of Lake District. (31 July 1880)

October 1880: The Mill Shuts Down for Good

The wait proved to be brief. The mill that had started up in July shut down for good only three months later. There was no chance of it ever reopening; the Bodie *Weekly Standard-News* reported that within weeks the mill was being torn down. On November 6 George Rowan placed a notice in the *Herald* stating that after July 5, 1881, he would "sell goods for cash only, except to such as give collateral security." All we can make of this eight-month lead time is that he may have expected to redeem scrip from the company until

July. Since Rowan was the town's largest merchant (and perhaps its largest creditor), no doubt he could see what lay ahead. He would need time to collect on his accounts, especially because many unemployed miners had only worthless scrip in their pockets. We can only wonder how much the company owed Rowan and whether he ever collected.

The Owens Valley *Inyo Independent* reported the situation in Mammoth City in its 30 October 1880 edition:

> We learn that about everybody is leaving Mammoth City. More than half the business houses are already closed up, and great depression prevails...a large portion of the late residents of Mammoth, however, are coming this direction to seek their fortunes.... The material of the defunct Mammoth *Times* newspaper is being removed to Bishop Creek...and that locality is soon to have a newspaper of its own....

The *Herald,* now the only newspaper in Lake District, replied in its next issue:

> It has been quite the style of late for our neighboring papers to give Mammoth a "black eye" whenever a chronic dead-broke grumbler or discharged miner chooses to pour his sorrows into the willing ears of their newsgatherers.... As to the removal of a number of business houses, the story is quite true, and it is also true that there has never been a time since ore was first struck on Mineral Hill that one well appointed and well managed store would not have been quite sufficient for the real needs of the community; but when the rich strikes were made, merchants rushed their goods in without reason—in some instances to the extent from $20,000 to $40,000—until there were no less than five leading stores and a proportionate allowance of small traders, hotels, saloons etc. The result has, of course, been disastrous to them, and many have moved and are moving their goods away—losers financially, but gainers in wisdom. As they have not generally been patrons of the Herald, we have no sympathy to waste on them.... (6 Nov. 1880)

Chapter 10 ಞ

COMPANY TOWN

If it seems strange that the *Mammoth City Herald* reported nothing about the importance of July 17, the date that assessments became delinquent, and nothing about the tailspin of company stock prices, perhaps the fact that Mammoth City was a company town explains the dearth of company news—particularly bad news. The company *was* the town. From the beginning it had been obvious that the company payroll was the lifeblood of the town and that the fate of the district was coupled to the fate of the company. It was clear that they would prosper—or fail—together. But it was not clear, until George Forbes spelled it out in plain language, just how the company and its principal superintendent, William Hardy, controlled the news and dominated the district. Forbes referred to Mammoth as a "One-Man Town" and then gave examples of the ways Hardy ran the town:

> Mr. Hardy, the Superintendent of the Mammoth Mine, runs it. When the poor man with a large family objected, quite naturally, I think, to having his house the focus of a blasting bombardment, he was discharged, had to sacrifice his little property and leave; the miner who concluded to open a boarding house and, unfortunately, at the same time made up his mind to draw a considerable amount of back pay found he had trod on the sure road to ruin as he also was discharged, and any employee of the Mammoth

Company forbidden to patronize him. The Company may be said to be the only disburser here, so far. (14 Jan. 1880)

Undoubtedly there was a great deal of secret chafing. There is only one instance of a merchant successfully fighting the superintendent. The mercantile firm of Gilson, Barbour and Company found themselves on the wrong side of the "autocratic Superintendent" when they asked for payment in cash instead of scrip, saying that their own creditors would not accept company scrip. Hardy forbade all Mammoth Company employees to patronize them. However, Gilson & Barbour fought back by going to court, a tactic that most who ran afoul of Mr. Hardy did not have the money for. Their suit against Hardy and the company called for heavy civil damages. Hardy, realizing that this one had gotten away from him and that his position was weak, backed off and rescinded his order.

Forbes also explained in great detail the failure of Bogart and Farnham's *Mammoth City Times*. His charges were never refuted.

We have all had the fact of newspaper suppression in France, Germany or Russia forced on our attention, and in those far-off lands the act seemed to be one of tyranny and unbearable oppression. It surely cannot be considered in any more favorable light in this land of liberty. The Czar of Mammoth has taken a hand in this kind of game without giving his opponent a chance to cut the cards. The *Times Review* published some articles without submitting the same to 'official' censorship. I am not disposed to enter into the merits of the case further than to say that in the absence of information from the company, some of the items published were perfectly reasonable. Where everything connected with a mine and mill is secret, something must be assumed. Mark the consequence to Bogart & Farnham. Their circulation was cut off by orders from the company's office, and an obligation purchased and enforced against them unrelentingly by tools of the same agency. Finding ruin staring them in the face, they offered to retract, but it was too late. They had to go and the *Times* comes out under new management. We presume that the new proprietors, having this example of the freedom of the press before their eyes, will work in the harness with docility in public, however they may chafe in secret. (14 Jan.1880)

None of these incidents, nor any pessimistic news about company finances were published in the Mammoth City newspapers.

MAMMOTH CITY HERALD.

Mammoth City, Wednesday, April 7.

TRAVELER'S GUIDE.

Ogg's Bodie Line.

Leaves Mammoth City for Bodie every morning at four o'clock.
Leaves Bodie for Mammoth daily on the arrival of the Carson Stage.

NOTICE.

From and after this date ALFRED MC-MILLAN will deliver the HERALD to subscribers in Mammoth City, Pine City and Mill City, and collect for the same.

LOCAL MINING ITEMS.

Mammoth.

We are enabled to give our readers official reports of the most favorable character this week with regard to the working and general outlook of this important enterprise. During the week ending Saturday last good headway was made in both Nos. 3 and 4 tunnels, notwithstanding three days' loss of time on account of the severe wind storm which made it impossible for the men to get to and from work. In No. 3 tunnel the work is being run south on the main header, which has been driven 25 feet, making a total length of 866 feet. The work now being done is all in a favorable looking vein formation. In tunnel No. 4, although but four days' was done during the week, 28 feet was accomplished, all in quartz. The general appearance of the vein is of a most encouraging character. The total length of this lower and deepest tunnel is now 1196 feet. The machinery is all working well.

H. L. & M. C. Joint Tunnel.

Work had to be suspended on this tunnel also for three days, partly on account of the storm and partly for repairs on the air compressor. Everything is working in the most satisfactory manner, and notwithstanding the short time and that the rock is somewhat harder than at the time of our last report, 21 feet headway was made, giving a total length of tunnel 626 feet.

Don Quixote Tunnel.

Superintendent Wallerstein is expecting orders from below in regard to the resumption of operations on this most promising property. It is a pity to have a mine with the rich developments recently made, lying idle, and it is to be hoped it will soon start up again. Everything points to the conclusion that but a short distance will have to be run before a rich body that is known to exist in

A DIFFERENCE OF OPINION.

Judge Eddy Rises to Explain a Point.

Being dissatisfied with our report of the part he took in the proceedings of the miner's meeting, Justice Eddy hands in the following note:

EDITOR HERALD:—In your report of the meeting of citizens and miners held at Giles' Hall on Thursday last, you state that I denounced in unmeasured terms the effort of the mining companies to reduce the wages, etc. I do not think you reported me correctly in what I said on that occasion; for while it is true that I did say something in opposition to the reduction of wages, I had much more to say in regard to the general management of the affairs of the Mammoth Company, and the vituperation that has been indulged in at various times by some of the leading men of that company in regard to the citizens of this district. It is a well known fact among the miners and others who have lived here nearly two years, that thousands upon thousands of dollars have been squandered by the bad management of the affairs of the Mammoth Company. Chutes and tramways that cost thousands of dollars were entirely useless, and there was not a practical man in the district but so expressed himself at the time they were being built. Some say if they have made mistakes and squandered money, whose business is it so long as they pay their bills? But I may ask who are THEY? It is every stockholder of the company, and I am one of them, and have as much right to criticise the management as any member of the company. If there is a man in this district, or ever has been, who has thrown any obstacles in the way of the Mammoth Company, by either word or deed, I have never heard of them. I challenge comparison between this and any other mining district on the Coast for the good order of its citizens, and yet they have been denounced in the vilest terms by some of those who have had a good deal to say about the management of the Mammoth Company. It may, perhaps, be useless for me to offer any suggestions or advice to those who manage the affairs of the Mammoth Company; but, nevertheless I propose to say a word on that subject: If they ever expect to make a success of the Mammoth mine, they had better send a good live man here as Superintendent, who knows something about a mine and the business connected therewith, and also knows how to treat people decently that he comes in contact with, and not try any more of their bulldosing games. I believe the

to besmirch, we will call attention to the work of and Monte Cristo companies the same individuals who Mammoth Company. In th most terrible Winter ever k Sierra Nevadas, these men capital and energy, have their works into Mineral Hil pose of developing their le depth. The opening of tho proves the value of the Mon for which you are applying That is to say, while they ar their money and energy i adverse circumstances for a which it is to be hoped will and may enrich you—whilst look on and see them do it, ing a dollar to the enterpris word of encouragement, but trary, allowing your voice a used in the interest of the w in the community—the cr neither weave nor spin. Do you are answered?

THE WEATHER

FAREWELL WINTER,
THE COMING SPR

Our Local Historian Indul
mynuisances and Digre
Pulls the Record on th
the Weather—Stories of
and the Hope of Comin
and Profits.

For severity and durati storm has had no equal du ceptionally severe season. of 1877–78, the snow fell v did not continue so long in by this time of the year t getting warm and pleasant, eral Park the snow had a peared, and heavy teams and running between this and was but shortly after this that Gen. Dodge, Mr. Lamb Clarke came in and negoti purchase of the Mammoth shortly afterward commence Geo. W. Rowan was movin stock of general merchand to arrive in this section.

Mammoth City Herald, 7 April 1880.

Forbes's revelations help us understand why both papers seldom published anything derogatory about the company. They also explain how the company could have concealed its financial problems in Mammoth. In addition, the company could hide its lack of cash behind its practice of paying workers once a month and then only in scrip. It is also possible that the editors themselves knew nothing of the company's precarious financial condition; company secrets probably were known only to a few officers. Forbes, from the safety of Los Angeles, could write about the company with impunity:

> The movements of the Mammoth Company are mysterious. Like the ways of the Lord, "they are past finding out." The simplest transactions are covered with an air of secrecy, and the workings of the mines are as secure, by report or observation from the public as is the meaning of any chapter of Revelations. No man in Mammoth could learn anything in regard to the bullion production till the San Francisco papers came to hand. It was and is the same with the rich rock so carefully sacked up for many weeks. Either the Mammoth has no mine or a very rich one. I incline to the latter opinion. (14 Jan. 1880)

And there it is again—the rich ore. Where did it go, and who got it? Not long after Forbes's blistering article, Superintendent Hardy left Mammoth City. He left while the mill was still running and just after a production report had been published in the *Herald*. By the time the news hit the camps, that the mill had closed for the winter and that there was no production, Hardy was gone. Is this an amazing coincidence, or did Mr. Hardy time his departure quite purposely and precisely?

Chapter 11 ∾

FIRE!

Whatever Mammoth City editors knew or didn't know, reported or didn't report, about the Mammoth Mining Company suddenly was of no importance at all. For on Sunday morning—it was November 14 of 1880—Mammoth City erupted in flames. Having often warned the unheeding populace about the all-too-likely possibility of fire, the *Mammoth City Herald*, to its horror, saw its worst prophecies come true just eight days after reporting the Republicans' exuberance over Garfield's victory. (All quotes that follow are from the November 20 edition.)

> At a few minutes past ten o'clock [Sunday] morning a fire was discovered in the roof of and near the front of Geo. Rowan's store. In a few minutes all the front of the store and the adjoining buildings presented a solid sheet of flame, which almost immediately communicated with the buildings opposite [jumping across Mammoth Avenue], and before people had time to realize the extent of the calamity, all the upper end of town was a sheet of seething, roaring flame.

The *Herald* office and the McAfee house, across the street from each other, were headquarters for fighting the fire, but the McAfee house was soon torn down to create a firebreak. On the opposite side of the street an empty 100-foot lot next to the *Herald* office on the up side provided a natural firebreak. Fortunately for the lower portion of the town, "the wind was very light at the time, blowing up the hill and from the Mammoth works."

After a "concerted effort," the fire on both sides of the street was halted at the breaks between the buildings. Fully half of Mammoth City was totally destroyed: three saloons, two hotels (including Franklin Buck's Standard Hotel), two lodging houses, one drug store, two meeting halls (one of them, the Magnolia Hall, housed the school), two general stores (one was George Rowan's, in which he lost over $10,000 worth of inventory), one stable, one shoe shop, and eighteen other structures listed as "cabin," "dwelling" or "building."

Only the school recovered quickly. As the *Herald* explained, "the school had been so ably conducted that it had gained a strong hold upon the parents and others interested in the progress of the little ones...." Classes resumed on Thursday, four days after the fire, in a room borrowed from Thomas Fahey on central Mammoth Avenue. The Odd Fellows donated benches; the Mammoth Mill, a blackboard and tables; others loaned or donated whatever they could and businessmen chipped in for much of the rest, including a stove, firewood and desks.

Chapter 12 ↩

THE END OF HOPE

Looking back at Lake District today through sentimental, gold-tint-ed glasses, we may drift into picturing it all as a romantic adven-ture—a high alpine camp amidst magnificent mountains where Republicans equalled Democrats and "real love making" occurred on weekends under the pines of Lake Mary. Although in some ways those mining days may seem idyllic, life was never easy. Most of the time fresh food was scarce and costly, winters were long and bitter cold, pay was low—but always, always there had been hope. However, during the summer and fall of 1880, one by one all rea-sons for hope vanished—and the fire was the final blow. Businesses lost thousands of dollars in inventories and property; miners lost their homes, their belongings, their livelihood and their dreams. None made any attempt to recover. With the Mammoth mines and mill shut down, the other mines producing little, and half the town destroyed by fire, there was little incentive to stay and no incentive at all to rebuild the town. Numbly, Lake District's people looked at the calendar and sighed: mid-November 1880, the first snow just around the corner and only bleak prospects ahead. Some talked of buying property and starting over, but that was only talk. Most left that winter, never to return, nor were their places filled by other souls eager to wrest the precious yellow metal from Mineral Hill. Mammoth City and the other three camps, like drought-stricken weeds, wilted and died that November.

"No Report Received"

On 22 January 1881, the column titled "Local Mining Items" in the *Mammoth City Herald* reflected the hard times. Under both of the headings, "Mammoth" and "H. L. & M. C. Joint Tunnel," were the stark words, "No report received." In this column, formerly filled with facts and figures about each tunnel's progress and hopes for the future, now was only the epitaph, "No report received."

In the same edition in an article titled "Half Sheet," the *Herald* lamented its own uncertain future:

> It is useless to attempt to disguise the fact that at this time business in Mammoth is almost at a standstill, and the income of the *Herald*, as a consequence, is not sufficient to keep up the publication of our four page edition without resorting to the 'doubling' of dead advertisements to occupy the surplus space; therefore the paper will be issued in the present form until Spring breaks, or until times are better—or worse.

(Doubling of dead ads was occurring as early as the 6 November 1880 edition. Out of a total of twenty columns, that issue duplicated four columns of ads.) Business hadn't just slowed down; it was close to a halt.

Three weeks after printing "Half Sheet," the *Herald* itself closed shop. On July 27 the post office shut its doors. The *Herald's* editor, William Barnes, eventually headed for Bodie to start a new paper. The *Bridgeport Chronicle-Union*, a rival newspaper, resented his move there, saying: "If this is the case, it will be an imposition upon the people of that town...." (5 May 1881). Nevertheless, the Bodie *Weekly-Standard News* reported on 21 December 1881 that William Barnes would issue a newspaper in Bodie called the *Evening Herald:* "His material is the same we believe as that which he employed on these various publications, all now deceased."

Sold by the Sheriff

The Mammoth Mining Company's inglorious finale occurred at a sheriff's sale in Mammoth City. On 6 July 1881 the Bank of California won a judgment against the company for $26,954.57 plus interest of seven percent on the unpaid balance. The bank, which as one of the company's largest creditors had foreclosed on the company, decided to sell the property for whatever it could get. In September the *Bridgeport Chronicle-Union,* under the headline "A Great Sacrifice," reported matter-of-factly on the death of the golden dream that was Lake District:

> The real estate and personal property of the Mammoth Mining Company recently sold by Sheriff [James] Showers [on August 26, 1881] went for less than a song. As a sample we may cite: 50 tons of soda sold for $1 a ton, and 32½ tons of salt brought $2.50 for the lot. The real estate—mine, etc. brought only $15,100; and the personal property, which was worth tens of thousands, brought only $7,211.88, and that is the way everything goes in a dead mining camp. The mine was held by the Bank of California; but the personal property was sold to different parties, the Bodie Tunnel Company being a large purchaser. (10 Sept. 1881)

While the bank recovered some, if not most, of its money, those who paid up to $20 a share for stock in the spring of 1879 received practically nothing on their investment. Nor did those who invested in Mammoth City real estate and business. "James Rice, postmaster, put over $7,700 into a hotel, post office, and barn...when the boom broke, he sold out for $200.00" (Ryan 1902).

Within three months of the sheriff's sale, the mill was being dismantled and ghosts were softly gliding in to take possession of the abandoned camps. In a roundup of county news for 9 November 1881, the Bodie *Weekly Standard-News* reported that only one business in Lake District, the sawmill, was still flourishing and that Mammoth City was almost deserted:

> Rowan's saw mill in Mammoth has been running out from 10,000 to 12,000 feet of lumber daily all summer, and has about 80,000 in the yard. Owing to the near approach of winter, the mill will

close down on Tuesday or Wednesday.... Mammoth City is almost deserted, the only business houses there being P. A. Wagner's store and brewery.... The Mammoth mill in Mammoth City is being torn down. The turning lathe, and also the air compressor that was used at the mine, is being boxed and will be shipped to Bodie.

Chapter 13

WHAT WENT WRONG?

We may never know the full answer to this tantalizing question about the Mammoth Mining Company. But young John Hays Hammond, an ambitious, 25-year-old mining engineer, thought he knew exactly what was going wrong and did not hesitate to tell the company as much: that their ore existed "in imagination only."

> From Bodie [1880], I proceeded to Mono Lake and then south to Mammoth, another center of mining excitement. The mines there also proved of slight value, and I so informed the owners, natural-ly to their disappointment. They had gone to the extent of erect-ing a mill in anticipation of ore that existed in imagination only. The worthlessness of the enterprise was apparent to any trained engineer and within a few months speculators and prospectors were moving on to other fields. (1935)

How much credibility should we give Hammond's opinion? Hammond had graduated from Yale and studied mining engineering at the Royal School of Mines in Freiberg, Germany, schooling far beyond that of many practical "engineers" of his day. He eventually became a successful and much honored consulting engineer. But in 1880 he had just returned from Europe and for all his schooling, he admittedly had no experience or training in quartz mining. He was employed as a "special expert" for the U.S. Geological Survey in 1880; probably it was in that capacity that he examined the Bodie and Mammoth mines. His assessment of the Bodie mines—"that few of them could be worked profitably and that the majority would have to shut down"—proved to be correct. The majority of the Bodie mines did shut down, although two of them operated profitably for many years. Was his opinion of the Mammoth mines also correct?

The Puzzle

With not a single financial report and no documented figures to help us determine what went wrong, we must piece together company finances as best we can, from comments and estimates that were made years after the company's demise. Two of our sources, Chalfant and Whiting, freely admit that they were unable to find reliable figures. They give us hearsay and rumor, and identify it as such, because that is all they could find; and they refrain from judging whether that hearsay is anywhere near the truth. The other source, John Ryan, writing twenty years later, bases his figures on "reliable authority," but never identifies that authority. The estimates from these three sources, although laced with uncertainty, are all that we have to go on. Contemporary newspapers, even those that were not beholden to the Mammoth Mining Company, need to be read with care. You will note that mining news, then and now, is often qualified with phrases such as "It is reported that..." or "The company says that..." or "It is said that...." What such qualifiers really mean is, "So-and-so said that the ore is worth a million dollars but I, the author of this piece, have no way of knowing whether what he says is true or 100 percent bunkum."

Keeping these cautions in mind, let us, then, review the reports and the hearsay and see if we can arrive at even a fuzzy picture of company finances and reasons for its failure. Fuzzy though the picture may be, we today have access to far more information than did Mammoth City residents; company secrecy and censorship kept them ignorant of company problems. Let us examine the reported numbers, with all their uncertainties, and try to judge their reliability; let us analyze what we know and don't know about company income and expenses and about its milling techniques; and let us review some theories about the company's failure. Here are the "facts," as best I could determine them. And here are what I consider some reasonable conclusions. If you don't agree with mine, you are welcome to form your own!

Capital Investment

How much capital did the company raise? We don't know. What did the company spend? Most estimates of the company's capital expenditures come close to those mentioned by Chalfant, about $385,000. "The Mammoth Company was said to have spent $160,000 on its mill, $125,000 in its mines, and $100,000 on roads and buildings" (1942). (Note his qualifier!) On what the company spent for operations—payroll, chemicals, freight, etc., we have no clues at all.

Income and Outgo

The first question that needs to be addressed is: how much gold and silver did the company produce? On this question Chalfant refrained from giving his own opinion, but noted that "there are great differences in estimates of what it recovered from the ore it worked" (1947). First he mentions an 1888 *California Journal of Mines and Geology* estimate of $200,000 total output. Undoubtedly this reference is based on or is the same as the article written by H. A. Whiting in the *Eighth Annual Report of the State Mineralogist.* The State Mining Bureau sent Whiting, a mining engineer, to Mono County in the summer of 1888 to gather information on mines. Whiting first tells why it is impossible to come up with firm figures and then says that the prevailing opinion of a few who had lived in Lake District (only a few remained in the area at the time he wrote his report, seven years after the mill closed) was about $200,000.

> Such bullion as has been produced from this district is reported to have been valued at from $7 to $16 per ounce; but as to the total bullion product from its mines it was found impossible to gather trustworthy statistics; all records had long since been removed and no one was found who could speak from any positive knowledge of the facts. Indeed, the very methods which appear to have been employed in shipping the product were such as to make the collection of information respecting its amount, exceedingly laborious, if

not altogether impracticable [could this have been deliberate on the part of the Mammoth Mining Company?]. The bullion was shipped not alone from Mammoth, but sometimes from Bodie or Benton, and one large lot of exceedingly rich ore was sent to San Francisco. Nearly all of the amount shipped from this district, however, was produced from the Mammoth mine; and the prevailing opinion of a few who lived in Mammoth City during the productive period, places the total output of that mine at about $200,000.

Chalfant also refers to "an engineer who examined the property in 1902 [who] credited one stope with $300,000, and said the company had produced $2,000,000." Unfortunately, Chalfant does not identify the engineer or the source for his estimates. Could it have been John Ryan?

Ryan said that "over $300,000 in free gold" was mined in just one section of tunnel two and he estimates that upwards of $500,000 was extracted from the property. Ryan's figures come from "Substance of a Report upon the Mammoth Mines," which he wrote in 1902. This report was never published but I have been privileged to see a copy. Ryan, a mining engineer, examined the mine and had assays made but nowhere does he name the "reliable authority" upon which he bases past production figures.

If $2 million in gold and silver were taken out of Mineral Hill during the few months the mill was in production (if you count up the months the mill was shut down for repairs, for lack of ore and for snow, you may find that it operated no more than perhaps twelve months total), it seems unlikely that the company would have gone bankrupt so soon. Two million dollars on a $385,000 investment in three years would have been a remarkable return and put the Mammoth mine in the big league. But what if the $2 million output is correct after all but was never reported to the stockholders? Could embezzlement on such a large scale have taken place? We'll get to that in a moment.

Profit or Loss?

Regardless of how much the mine produced, the second question that needs to be answered is: did the company operate at a profit or a loss? If the company had made a sizable profit, the stockholders should have received a share. Surely the local papers would have headlined any such payments, yet there is no mention that the stockholders ever received anything.

To determine profitability, we would need to know ore values and production costs—and both figures are elusive. The samples that reportedly assayed $35,000 or more a ton tell us nothing about average value. Bill Chalfant, who was well acquainted with miners and prospectors all his life, had learned to be skeptical of such samples. His warning is worth heeding, whether we are reading the *Mammoth City Times* or a current promotion piece. "The experienced reader need not be reminded of the prospector's tendency to feature the richest-looking piece of ore, though it be no larger than half a golf ball in size" (1947). One report to the *Mining and Scientific Press* (preceded by the newspaper's disclaimer, "We admit, unendorsed, opinions of correspondents") stated, "The ore from the croppings of this lode assays, on an average, $30 per ton. The cost of reduction and extraction is probably $5, leaving a net yield of $25 per ton" (19 April 1879). According to the local papers, the Mammoth's tunnels, notably tunnel two, occasionally produced ore assaying $50 to $60 a ton, but that seems to have been considerably above the average grade. In the opinion of John Ryan, "the average for all the workings [that he saw in 1902] was in excess of $10 a ton."

Let us consider bullion production figures of $200,000 and $500,000. Whatever they might have been, for lack of cost figures, we have no way of knowing whether revenue was more than eaten up by production costs or whether it produced some profit. We do know that the company was forced to borrow from the Bank of California to keep operating. If in three years the mines were not producing enough to pay the investors a dividend and not even enough to pay current bills, that would seem to indicate a loss—not a profit—and that alone would be a plausible explanation for closing the mines. If indeed this was the case, the lack of return—from ledges that were heralded as so promising—might be explained in part by the company's mining and milling practices. The company literally threw away a significant portion of the precious metals the men worked so hard for, in the dumps of the mines and in the tailings from the mill.

Mining and Milling Practices

The company only worked ore that was worth $20 a ton or more, dumping ore worth anything less. This may indicate that costs were high and that they could not work lower grade ore profitably; or it may indicate a major mistake and an extravagant waste of some potentially profitable ore. According to Ryan, "assays of old tailings show that practically only free gold was reclaimed when the...ores were worked, the saving not over 40 percent, and the waste carried better values than the original ore of many big mines of the present." A brief look at standard milling techniques of the 1880s will explain how this could have happened.

Ore entering the upper floor of the Mammoth's mill was dropped over a large grate, often called a grizzly, that sorted the rock. The finer ore fell into the ore bins, while the coarser rock went first to a crusher and then to the bins. From the bins, ore moved down to the stamps. After the stamps pounded the ore to powder or *pulp,* water was fed into each mortar to hold the pulp in liquid suspension. Then the millman, with a wooden spoon, added just the right amount of mercury (quicksilver), which combined chemically with the gold and silver in the pulp to produce an *amalgam* (an alloy of mercury and another metal).

> Gold alloyed with an appreciable amount of silver requires a larger addition of quicksilver than does a purer gold. One ounce of gold of average fineness can be amalgamated with 1 oz. of quicksilver, but for a safety margin, an allowance must be made, so that 2 ozs. will answer better; and with extremely divided gold, $2^1/_2$ or 3 ozs. (California State Mining Bureau, 1895)

Up to this point in the milling process, little or no gold or silver was lost. The next step involved running the amalgam over copper plates (called *aprons*) to which the amalgam would readily adhere. During this step critical losses of gold and silver could take place—losses ranging as high as forty or sixty percent. The same Mining Bureau publication describes how this could occur:

Stamps and mortars of a California mill, 1890s; aprons in the foreground. The pulverized ore, mixed with water and mercury, flowed from the mortars down over the aprons' copper plates. The mercury, which had picked up some of the gold and silver to form gold-rich amalgam, adhered to the aprons.

If, as was formerly the almost universal custom, the lower end of the apron be contracted (and in numerous cases this contraction was as great as four to one), the depth of the pulp spread over the surface of the plate increases as it passes down; the flow of the water across a given section becomes uneven, forming at the sides a swirl, along the edge of which, sand is precipitated, covering and rendering that portion of the plate useless, from its inability to come into contact with the particles of amalgam, while producing scouring currents at other parts.... The liquid pulp, starting with a width equal to that of the mortar discharge, is made to pass over sluiceplates from 1' to $2^1/_2$' in width; hence the comparatively small percentage of amalgam obtained from them.

The waste (water and pulp amalgam that did not adhere to the plates) then was channeled downhill and presumably washed into the nearest creek. The amalgam on the plates was gathered and then retorted (a heating process that drove off the mercury); the

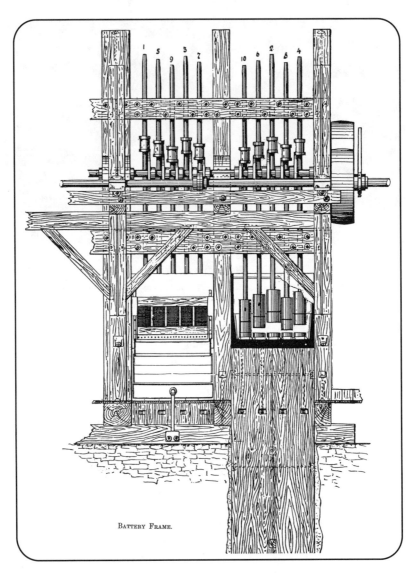

BATTERY FRAME.

A battery consisted of a stamp and a mortar; the stamp, weighing up to 900 pounds or more, dropped into the mortar, crushing the ore that moved continuously into it. This drawing shows ten batteries, the cam shaft, and the heavy timbering required for a battery frame. The mudsills are 14" x 16" pine; the linesills 12" x 16" pine, the battery posts 12" x 24" and 20" x 24" pine. (Drawings above and opposite from *Eighth Annual Report of the State Mineralogist, 1888*)

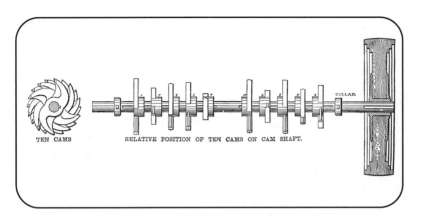

TEN CAMS   RELATIVE POSITION OF TEN CAMS ON CAM SHAFT.

This cam shaft is 14 feet long, $5^1/_2$ inches in diameter and is made of wrought iron or soft steel. Cam placement on the shaft, the height of the stamps, and the sequence of drop were critical, for the weight of the stamps had to be distributed evenly as they were raised by the cams. The order of drop was: 1, 8, 4, 10, 2, 7, 5, 9, 3 and 6. The cams were fastened to the shaft by steel, hand-fitted keys. The cam-shaft pulley was driven by a 16-inch-wide, 5-ply rubber belt.

remaining gold and silver were run into bars for shipment. According to the *Engineering and Mining Journal*, the "bars that have been turned out...ranged from 900 to 966 fine; the percentage of silver...from 70 to 30 per cent" (Jan.–June 1879).

An article in the *Mining and Scientific Press* indicates that a goodly portion of the Mammoth mill's gold and silver may have gone into the tailings and down the creek. "Only free gold was saved from these ores, and no attempt was made to concentrate these ores, which is the real road to success in mining in this region. Samples returned from the tailings are said to have returned a good percentage of sulphurets [sulfides], high in gold and silver" (30 April 1904). Whiting, too, mentioned that no provision "seems to have been made in this mill to concentrate and save the pyritic minerals in the tailings. Samples of such concentrates, crudely separated by hand panning from the arrastra tailings, are reported to have given high assay returns both in gold and silver...." (1888). Ryan said much the same, adding, "The mining and milling was confined to the oxidized free ores. These were practically exhausted by the spring of 1881."

The Price of Gold

To appreciate the significance of ore values, and in order to compare mining production today with yesterday, we need to remember that the values of gold and silver have fluctuated dramatically over the past one hundred years. During the time of Lake District, the price of gold stayed close to $20 an ounce. In 1934 the U.S. Treasury fixed the price of gold at $35 an ounce. In recent years the price has ranged from $300 to $600 an ounce. Silver values too have changed. In the late nineteenth century one ounce of gold was worth 22 ounces of silver. Today the ratio of gold to silver is more than 40. If a ton of ore produced an ounce of gold in 1879, it brought $20. Today that ounce would bring around $400.

Did They Quit Too Soon?

Some thought so. Henry DeGroot, a mining engineer from the State Mining Bureau, visited the district in 1890 and reported his findings in the *Tenth Report of the State Mineralogist*. He mentioned that in the opinion of some mining experts (note that this is not his opinion) the mill "never ought to have been shut down, and that under a proper management it could even now be started up and run with profit...in their judgment the Mammoth Company abandoned their enterprise too soon. Certain it is, much ore that would not pay eight or ten [dollars a ton] could now be worked with remunerative results...." Ryan, too, felt the mines still had potential. He estimated ore values at $9 a ton and mining and milling costs at $3 a ton.

These prophecies have yet to come true. Through the years many have explored for ore and worked it using other processes and modern techniques. But although small amounts of gold and silver have been recovered, along with lesser amounts of copper and lead, the big bonanza—if it's there—has yet to be tapped.

Some Other Theories

Several other explanations of the mine's closure circulated locally. One attributed the shutdown to a lack of chemicals at the mill, particularly quicksilver. Another blamed the painful and debilitating paralysis that struck General Dodge in 1878, rendering him nearly speechless, mentally deranged and unable to continue his role as prime mover and organizer of the Mammoth Mining Company. Another speculated that company officers were not willing to endure the severe winters, the isolation and the hardships in order to keep an eye on dishonest superintendents and miners, who may have waxed rich while the mines failed. While some rejected this latter explanation as sheer speculation, stealing ore—*highgrading* they called it—was a common practice throughout the mining country. And why not?

Highgrading

By any standard, wages were low. Although we have no firm figures for wages in Lake District's mines, Mark Twain in *Roughing It* cites some figures for Virginia City around 1863. He received $10 a week as a quartz-mill worker, before being offered $25 a week to become the city editor of the *Daily Territorial Enterprise*. He noted that in the larger mines employing hundreds of men "[l]aboring men's wages were four and six dollars a day, and worked in three 'shifts' or gangs...." My grandfather, a carpenter in Virginia City in the late 1890s, told of miners receiving $4 for a ten-hour day.

In Lake District the Mammoth Mining Company paid its employees on the first Friday of each month, usually in scrip, not cash. Whatever his daily wage, no miner was going to get rich mining for scrip—unless he happened to be working in tunnel two when they struck a pocket of highgrade ore, such as the day they found ore reportedly worth $87,000 a ton. Some ore rich in free gold, when struck with a hammer, does not shatter but slowly comes apart in one's hand, being held together by spider-web-like filaments of pure gold. A few ounces of ore like that in one's pocket would bring as much as two weeks' pay!

With wages low and living costs high, it seems not at all unlikely that some miners—and perhaps superintendents?—took advantage of opportunities to augment their $3 or $4 a day with a few ounces of free gold or a pound or two of ore. In fact, California's early miners considered highgrading a miner's right, a compensation for the hazards of mining. Even if he were caught, there was no way to establish that the ore in his pocket came from a specific location; and, most important, no mining camp jury would convict a miner with "specimens" in his pocket. Both Ryan and Tom Rigg (in his letters to Adele Reed) repeated tales of rich ore being stolen:

> It was said by old timers in the camp that hundreds of thousands of dollars worth of high grade ore were stolen by miners, sacked and packed on burros across the Minarets. There is a claim of little value credited with producing rich ore that was taken out westerly. Another story, accepted by old timers, is that 50 sacks of ore, stolen and taken to Nevada for reduction, netted over $50,000. Probably the total value of the stolen ore has been overestimated, nevertheless, there remains good reason to know that the value of such ore ran into many thousands of dollars. (Ryan 1902)

> The old Mammoth Mine was a 'get rich quick', they played stockholders instead of the mine, like many others. They spent a lot of money and when they did get a bunch of bonanza ore, they never got a nickel of it, it was all stolen. The Supt. and his gang got most, the 'trusties' got what they could. The head of the old company was known on the S.F. Stock exchange as 'Bilky Adams'. Everything was stock then, you paid for laundry, meals and so on. Charlie Albright used to get $20 a day and the tailings for rent of a 'spring-pole' mortar he had. After the company went broke, the Bank of Calif. took it over and let leasers work for nearly a year. Then the Bank closed everything and the camp blew up.

> Old Tom Agnew was recorder of the North Fork District around Agnew Meadows, Shadow and Minaret Creeks and the head of the San Joaquin. He told me he saw about 20 sacks of the bonanza ore in the [superintendent's] office one day, some open. Being a friend of the clerk he asked for a piece to assay. Tom said it went about $20,000 [a ton] in gold and $40,000 in silver, pretty good pickings for Bilky and his pals! (Reed 1982)

Chapter 14 ↷

WHAT *REALLY* WENT WRONG?

Are there any other explanations about why the Mammoth Mining Company shut down their mines and mill? Indeed there are.

What was the "game" Franklin Buck had in mind when he wrote that "the mine is not run to put the stock up but for some other game is kept back"? Was it anything like the game that correspondent George Forbes was thinking about when, almost a year before the mill closed, he mentioned "gross mismanagement, pointing to a freeze-out game"? Forbes was referring to a practice, not unknown today, in which key officers or directors would arrange a temporary or phony loss in order to buy out other stockholders at rock-bottom prices. As examples of mismanagement, he cited the waterworks on Lake Mary and the tramway:

> [Lake Mary] was dammed at a heavy outlay, without any beneficial result. An expensive chute for bringing down ore was erected on trestlework about strong enough to afford a secure rest for the long stem of a Turkish chibouk. Of course it blew down. (14 Jan. 1880)

The tramway was such an obvious fiasco that Forbes, like others, ultimately concluded that "the mill should have been built at the mine...." A less abrasive, but even more damning opinion came from Joseph Wasson, a mining writer of note and Mono County's assemblyman: the company "was a very hurried organization to say the least, and a mill was built before it was ascertained that there was ore to justify such a very considerable expenditure...." *(Mammoth City Herald* 3 Sept. 1879)

It is possible, of course, that the Mammoth Company's officers sincerely believed they had a good mine but that it did not live up to their expectations. Perhaps all the "reports" of rich ore were mostly hype and hope and fantasy, common diseases of miners. Mines and oil wells that don't prove up are nothing new; mining continues to be among the riskiest of ventures. Perhaps all the questionable decisions and the mismanagement—repeated shutdowns to repair the mill, doubling the stamps, installing a steam plant, losing the boiler down Sherwin Grade and the never-solved problem of building a reliable tramway that would keep the mill supplied with ore—were due to honest mistakes and bad luck, costing officers and directors severe losses on their own investments in the company. Perhaps General Dodge's illness compounded the mismanagement. Perhaps the San Francisco financiers themselves were deceived when they came to look at the claims in 1877. Chalfant suggested that the rich samples that initially attracted investors might not have come from the Mammoth tunnels at all, but "were lifted from Bodie deposits" (1935).

On the other hand, the records show that the company's founders were experienced in organizing and financing mining companies. Perhaps the operation was a fraud from beginning to end. Perhaps some of the stockholders were part of "the gang" that Tom Rigg referred to and neglected to pay their assessments because they had already shared in the "profits" skimmed off by the officers or the superintendent. Or perhaps the company was a stock scam, with the mines and the mill a come-on for suckers, the original holders selling off their own stock and cashing in early in the game when the price was high. If that was the case, then the poorly located mill and the rickety tramway are more understandable, not as part of a legitimate operation but only part of the glitz to dupe gullible investors.

Or perhaps it was the superintendent who was the villain of this story, either alone or in collusion with company officers. With the town as well as all operations under his control, he easily could have highgraded ore or falsified production records for the benefit of himself and company officers.

"The Mammoth Swindle"

A writer for the San Francisco *Daily Exchange* had no doubts at all about what really went wrong at the Mammoth, and he didn't hesitate to express his opinion bluntly and forcefully. This headline and his column were reprinted in the Candelaria (Nevada) *True Fissure* on 23 April 1881 as follows:

> About four years ago General George S. Dodge got an inkling that there was "a solid mountain of gold quartz" lying somewhere up back of the Yosemite, and being then in good health, he one day started up the country to see it. After a terrible journey he arrived on the spot in company with a lot of old prospectors. It was indeed a mountain. It was a mammoth mountain, and the General promptly christened it "Mammoth." The quartz from the croppings looked fine, and even if it was not very rich the General said it would do "to make a deal on." (The General used to make deals in those days and was regarded an accomplished dealer.) On behalf of himself and others, among them an innocent old party by the name of Lambeth, a bargain was made, and in due time a company was organized. Work was begun on the croppings, and some of the General's lieutenants were judiciously set to work in the lower levels on Pine street. It was regarded as the greatest favor imaginable in those days to get a smell of Mammoth at $3 a share. One had to have influence with the General or at least with Johnny Landers, who was enthusiastic over the property, and honestly so, we believe, to have even a proposition to buy entertained. Fabulous was the amount of pay rock in sight. There was a perfect mountain of it; and the sides of the mountain were so high and so steep all one had to do was to put in a blast, touch her off, and fill a dozen cars with falling fragments. These were to be run to the mill at a cost of a cent a ton. Water was there by the lake-full, and great forests of pine were there to furnish fuel at the cost of cutting. It was a magnificent scheme. After supplying a pretty fair share of the stock to the public at $3 per share, the "Company" thought it could afford to levy an asessment. It did so, and put up a twenty stamp water mill to reduce the mountain of gold into bullion. For a while the "Company" lay on its oars, and nothing

was heard of it. One day there came riding into Benton, California, on a reeking charger, a young man named Burke, who was employed about the mine. He bore a Sack—not a Nevada Sack—but a sack of gold quartz so rich that it fairly gleamed. The young man said that it came from the Mammoth. Attired as he was, in brown canvas and woolen, he suddenly appeared in Johnny Landers' office with the sack. He spread it out and was soon surrounded and eagerly questioned by the $3 brigade. He told his story modestly. One by one the $3 men slid out on the street. In an hour Mammoth was selling for $7 per share, Professor Saul and Herr Von Nathan bidding vociferously for it. The story grew as it traveled, and next day Mammoth was very scarce at $10. The big fish began to nose the bait and on[e] by one they bit. Robert Barton took 1,000 at $10^1/_2$; George Grayson got something like 5,000, in job lots, at from $11 to $15, and Thomas Bell ditto, ditto. Others got hooked and were reeled in fine style. About that time some $3 chaps appeared in new Spring suits. The genial and handsome Secretary came out with a watch chain a fathom long, and a diamond collar button as big as a burglar's bull's-eye. Poor General Dodge lay upon a bed of sickness, and apparently took no interest in the proceedings. He said feebly that "he always knew it was a good mine, and hoped his friends would make some money. As for him he did not have any further ambition in this world than to depart from it with a clear conscience." Meantime the new syndicate of capitalists put their heads together and resolved to develop the mine for all it was worth. They spent their money like water. They added twenty stamps to the mill, put in a $40,000 engine and boiler, built a $15,000 railway, dug three tunnels, and the Lord knows what. One day they started the mill on the rich rock. They ran it a month—forty stamps. When they cleaned up there was less than $20,000 in bullion. This was a set back, but they kept on. They hunted for richer ore, but they never found it. From that day to this there have been a series of assessments. The "mine" has now been abandoned. The men are all discharged, the machinery is lying in the snow rusting out, the camp is deserted. The last chapter in the farce is a twenty-five cent assessment, which it is hoped somebody will be innocent enough to pay, in order to clear up the Company's debts.

Chapter 15 ⌘

TAILINGS

With this chapter heading borrowed from a column in the *Mammoth City Times*, we near the end of this story about Lake District's camps and its people. Mammoth City was a typical hard-rock western mining camp, similar—though on a much smaller scale—to her sister towns nearby, Bodie, Aurora and Virginia City. Their miners came from everywhere, from many states and several continents, and included a large proportion of foreign-born. They supported schools and other worthy projects. The camps owed their existence to precious metals, booming when they were first discovered and then busting when the ore gave out. Some, like Mammoth City, "busted sooner," succumbing quickly and quietly when economic signals pointed to lower yields and dull days ahead. Many camps suffered destructive fires, but some, Virginia City for example, quickly rebuilt and their mines continued to produce. In Mammoth City, where confidence in the future was as rare as the gold that was supposed to come out of Mineral Hill, fire was sudden death.

In the years following the Mammoth Mining Company's collapse, mining never completely petered out. Prospectors and small miners drifted in and drifted out. That occasional miners like Old Charley could scratch out a living indicated that, at the very least, low-grade ore was still there for the working. Lessees worked the

Mammoth and Lisbon mines intermittently. Whiting noted that since 1884 the lessees "mine during the winter months, and during the summer season they work the ore in an arrastra, at Pine City" (1888). I have investigated a Pine City arrastre, perhaps the very one Whiting refers to, and calculated that its diameter was between seven and nine feet. Although the water wheel and most of the arrastre have disappeared, the curved scarrings from fragments of the drag stones and the floor stones were the key to estimating its size.

In the summer of 1885 a steam-powered, five-stamp mill was built at the Lisbon mine, whose ore was yielding $20 a ton in gold. A 300-foot tramway connected mine and mill. Off and on, work continued at the Headlight, the Monte Cristo, and some of the other mines. Altogether, Lake District's population was counted in tens, not hundreds. The *Bridgeport Chronicle-Union* for 8 November 1884 reported a total of five votes, all Democratic, cast in Lake District for the general election that year.

These intermittent mining activities did not arrest the rapid decay of Mammoth City. Only seven months after the Sheriff's sale in August 1881, the March 8 Bodie *Weekly Standard-News* printed a bleak description of the camp.

> A person just in from Mammoth City states that the town has as much of a deserted look as one of the ancient towns of Mexico. There are but half-a-dozen people in the place and some days there are not that many. What few buildings remain standing are inhabited by frozen lizards, horned toads and coyotes. The snow is very deep. Decay and demoralization is apparent throughout the district. At one time Mammoth gave promise of being a large and prosperous camp. But it has gone the way of many other towns on this coast, and it is now only an echo of "what might have been." (1882)

By the time a reporter for the *Bodie Daily Free Press* visited Lake District three years later, the camps had faded into ghostly ruin.

> Not a soul to be seen in the old town of Mammoth. Houses overthrown by wind; tables, chairs, beds, etc. in wild confusion. Roofs breaking and broken down under weight of snow; clanging doors and shattered windows showing the deserted interiors. The once lively streets are filled with broken odds and ends incident to a hasty departure. The old Mammoth mill and battery and pan

© Stephen H. Willard

The Doyle stamp mill and cabin, Mammoth City c. 1930. Dr. Guy Doyle and associates built this mill around 1895, hauled the Knight wheel up from Mill City to provide the power and worked the mines a couple of years. Avalanches and heavy snow eventually demolished the buildings.

room has caved in upon the machinery. Office, stables, boarding houses are in good condition. An immense lot of wood lies piled at the foot of the tramway and mill. Mineral Park and Pine City present the same appearance as described above. The snow is from 4 to 5 ft. deep, and on the big lake is 3 ft. with 4 ft. of ice. Boats of all kinds lie half buried on the banks.... (March 1885)

When Henry DeGroot, a state geologist, visited the district in 1890, he noted that the mill had "gone to decay," the houses and outbuildings erected for the workmen had been "crushed into shapeless ruins by the weight of the snow," and parts of the tunnels had caved in.

The Doyle Mill

In 1895 Judge Robert Doyle of Chicago, with his son Dr. Guy Doyle, came to see the mining claim he had bought sight unseen. He had put up the money to build facilities and start operations.

Judge Doyle took one look and caught the next train back to Chicago. But young Guy became fascinated with mining and worked the Mammoth for a couple of years with Col. L. S. Judd, who served as superintendent. They built a small mill below tunnel four, a modern six-tank cyanide plant, a tramway, boarding house, bunkhouse, mine office, and assay office complete with furnace. Their twenty men reportedly struck ore worth $100 a ton. The post office reopened in July 1896, a sure sign of optimism. The mill was a marvel. Its ten stamps were powered by the same six-foot Knight wheel that had turned the flywheel at the Mammoth mill. Moved up to the Doyle mill, it now operated under a 57-foot head of water. The water came from Lake Mary in a ditch and a 22-inch steel pipeline. Ryan noted in his report that "by extending the pipe about 1000 feet further could get a head of 150 feet." The crushed ore was processed in the cyanide plant, one of the first in the United States. The cyanide process made it possible to mill lower grade ore than the Mammoth Company had milled and to recover more of the gold and silver. At some point, Dr. Guy discovered that the claim had been salted and snowshoed to Bridgeport to confront the men who had sold it to his father. They were, of course, long gone. Meanwhile, down at the old mill site, J. S. Cain removed ten stamps for a mill at Bodie.

But even with this new technology, the Mammoth mine did not operate profitably. Doyle and Judd had a falling out and the property was placed in receivership in August 1897. The post office closed in September 1898. Years later the Doyle mill was demolished by an avalanche. R. D. "Doc" Owen of Bishop acquired the mining property around 1928. A. E. Beauregard bought the claims from Owen in 1939.

John Ryan's Candles Won't Burn

John Ryan's 1902 report has been a valuable source of information on the Mammoth mine, as you can tell by the numerous times I have quoted it. But it has presented its own puzzles. Who hired Ryan to make the report and why? What are the sources of his information? Who is the "reliable authority" on which he bases his

H. W. Mendenhall c. 1910

This is the oldest known photograph of the Mammoth mill. For many years the photographer, Harry Mendenhall, had a photo studio in Big Pine.

past production figures? Now that we are acquainted with Guy Doyle, these questions become even more tantalizing. Could it have been Dr. Doyle who hired Ryan to investigate the mine? Was he thinking of selling it? By 1902 did Doyle still own an interest in the mine or had he lost it completely? Or was Ryan hired by someone who was interested in buying the claims from Doyle, or from whomever they had passed to? Whatever the answers to these questions, Dr. Doyle accompanied John Ryan into the mine workings and saved the day with his kerosene lantern!

The following passages in Ryan's report describe his investigation of tunnel one and the Folk claim, in company with Dr. Doyle:

> In order to work their property to the best advantage, the Mammoth Company had to run their workings through the Folk claim; this work opened up the Folk property, and incidentally proved the continuance to depth of the immense croppings that are to be seen on all of these claims, and can be seen for over two (2) miles....
>
> The air being so bad that I could not remain long enough to examine carefully, and my candles would not burn but Dr. Doyle

who had a kerosene lantern went on to the end of the tunnel and found end dry for about 75 feet from the end where the water came in....

There being no ladder in place, I was unable to gain entrance to these workings but I learned after leaving the property, from a party who worked the mine and took out the ore, that there was an upraise in the Mammoth ground by which I could have reached these workings. I consider my authority as to the workings absolutely reliable.... I am satisfied there is a vast amount of ore in these claims, the croppings are simply immense, and all carry gold, and in some places good values.

Later Years

The sturdy Knight water wheel rested for a few years but then powered a different type of enterprise when Charles Wildasinn sledded it down to the meadow and hooked it up to generate electricity for the small hotel he built in the early 1900s. Wildasinn owned meadow land and forest land, ran a sawmill on Mammoth Creek, and also filed for patents on some mining claims.

Short-lived revivals of the Mammoth, Lisbon and Monte Cristo have occurred from the 1930s to the present. The most recent operator is the Mammoth Lakes Mining Corporation, which worked some new veins as well as the adit of tunnel three. Don Beauregard, vice-president, has been an invaluable source of information.

Some numbers are on record for production and values in the district since Mammoth Mining Company days. Dean Rinehart and Don Ross, who mapped the geology of the Mount Morrison Quadrangle, compiled the data available and found it scarce.

> Data on later production are scant; the Mammoth mine produced 250 ounces of gold and 136 ounces of silver from 1896 to 1897 and 39 ounces of gold and 1,214 ounces of silver from 1939 to 1941. Most of the silver was produced in 1941 together with 4,768 pounds of copper and 28,388 pounds of lead. Also during the period 1939–41 the Monte Cristo mine yielded 1,153 ounces of gold and 18,606 ounces of silver that totaled $53,000 in value. (U.S. Geol. Survey 1964)

They found that during the 1939–1941 period, when several mines operated, the ore ran "about a third to half an ounce of gold and

The flywheel and rock foundation are all that is left to mark the location of the Mammoth Mining Company's stamp mill. At the site, by looking at old photos of the mill, you can picture exactly where it stood relative to the flywheel.

9 ounces of silver per ton." They also refer to Evans B. Mayo, a geologist with the State Division of Mines who studied the Mammoth Consolidated mine as well as some other old mines. He stated that "the average assays on some of the veins show values of about $12 per ton in gold over a width of six feet."

The magnificent Mammoth Lakes Sierra that yesterday lured the gold seekers today draws city folk seeking high mountain wilderness and alpine beauty. Sightseers, fishermen, hunters, backpackers, hikers, campers and photographers throng the campgrounds and trails in summer. Skiers flock to Pumice (Mammoth) Mountain's deep snow in winter. Today's speculators deal not in mining stock and gold bars but in real estate, mortgages and condos.

Miners often dug their foundations into the earth, piled up rocks for the side walls and roofed them with canvas or shakes. Although overgrown with brush, stone foundations like this are still recognizable near Mammoth City.

Time to Stop

For any author it is important to know when to stop. And so, I'm stopping—well, winding down. Writing in my cabin above Lake Mary, in a second-story loft, I am close to the mines and the camps and all their stories. I look across to Red Mountain where the ball-crusher used to clank and growl all night long. Reclaiming and interpreting what few bits and pieces remain of Mammoth's early mining history has been a joyous adventure. Original research and archaeological surveys have made it possible to fit some of the pieces together and to find others thought to be lost. Even now I am preparing a report on an archaeological excavation at Pine City. I look forward to discovering more new information and I continue to hope that Alfred McMillan's photographs will yet come to light. Much of the material in this book will then need to be re-examined and reinterpreted, probably leading to future revised editions.

A prospector's cabin, Lake District. Round nails indicate that this cabin was built after 1890. Heavy snows have collapsed the roof and continue to push the cabin walls sideways.

One More Thought

If you, the reader, be of a contemplative or romantic persuasion, I have one suggestion. Before you leave the Mammoth country, on a late afternoon as the shadows lengthen, wander up to Panorama Dome above Mammoth City and find some soft earth where you can sit comfortably. And listen. And reflect, as you look at the red slope across the ravine, that it was once touted as "the largest bonanza outside Virginia City." As George Hendricks noted in his *The Bad Man of the West,* it was a time and a spirit "that never were anywhere else before nor since nor ever will be again." It was in this small valley—not so long ago, really, only four generations back—that a thriving mining camp for a short time boasted a population of 1500 souls and echoed with the sounds of miners' drills, teamsters' oaths, dynamite explosions and stamps pounding. A camp where Republicans equalled Democrats and "real love making" occurred on weekends under the pines of Lake Mary.

So quickly did it vanish that now we are lucky if we can find the barest remnants of Pine City and Mammoth City and Mill City and Mineral Park. Remnants such as crumbling stone foundations. Weathered boards half hidden in the dirt and overgrowth. Square nails twisted and bent, bits of crockery caked with sand. Fragments of fuzed glass—green, blue, purple. Lengths of pipe and railroad track, twisted and rusted. A cemetery, its graves vandalized and its dead now nameless and forgotten. Crumpled ore cars. Dumps on the steep talus slope marking now-collapsed portals into the mines. Rotting timbers. Today the few cars on the dusty road, the occasional sightseers, the songs of birds, the sighing of the wind and the timeless rippling of the creek barely disturb the ruin and decay.

Mark Twain, more than a hundred years ago, vividly described the sudden death of a once-lively mining camp as only one could who had experienced it:

You may see, in places, its grassy slopes and levels torn and guttered and disfigured by the avaricious spoilers of fifteen and twenty years ago. You may see such disfigurements far and wide over California—and in some such places, where only meadows and forests are visible—not a living creature, not a house, no stick or stone remnant of a ruin, and not a sound, not even a whisper to disturb the Sabbath stillness—you will find it hard to believe that there stood at one time a fiercely flourishing little city, of two thousand or three thousand souls, with its newspaper, fire company, brass band, volunteer militia, bank, hotels, noisy Fourth of July processions and speeches, gambling hells crammed with tobacco smoke, profanity, and rough-bearded men of all nations and colors, with tables heaped with gold dust sufficient for the revenues of a German principality—streets crowded and rife with business—town lots worth four hundred dollars a front foot— labor, laughter, music, dancing, swearing, fighting, shooting, stabbing—a bloody inquest and a man for breakfast every morning— everything that delights and adorns existence—all the appointments and appurtenances of a thriving and prosperous and promising young city—and now nothing is left of it all but a lifeless, homeless solitude. The men are gone, the houses have vanished, even the name of the place is forgotten. In no other land, in modern times, have towns so absolutely died and disappeared, as in the old mining regions of California. (Clemens 1872)

As you listen and reflect, if you think that you hear an echo from that not so distant past, perhaps you do. Even such a no-nonsense reporter as George Forbes suggested that Mammoth's gold was as much romance as hard fact.

> The last thing at night, the first thing in the morning is gold, gold. You dream of ledges seamed with the precious metal; see huge bricks of it piled around you while lying in a dreamy, comatose state, and seem to inhale the yellow liquid with your waking breath.... (9 Feb. 1880)

And maybe, just maybe, the gold is still there. John Ryan concluded his 1902 report with a firm opinion. Will he yet be proved right?

> I would advise running crosscuts in all the tunnels (to the right) until the Main Vein is cut, when good values will unquestionably be encountered. All indications are favorable...a careful study of the lay of the vein and the ground, cannot but convince anyone that this is a large and valuable property, that it has been badly managed, and with proper development will make a big mine.

As for me, I am content to keep on filling that folder labeled "More Stuff" and to let George Forbes have the last word, as he wrote in the *Evening Express* on 9 February 1880:

> These notes like everything else must come to an end. They could have been much more full and continuous, but I have a horror of being considered tedious. Being interested in my work and knowing that I am not a proper judge of my own child, I am well prepared to believe that many digressions were superfluous. If the readers of this paper do not arise in their might and annihilate me, I may come before them again when anything worthy of note comes across the "ken" of my vision. No thanks, please.

A SELF-GUIDED TOUR OF LAKE DISTRICT'S GHOST TOWNS

I hope this half-day overview of the old mining camps will entice you to spend many hours or days at each site—wondering, wandering, and picturing all that happened here during the boom days more than a century ago. One special request: if in your wanderings you should come upon the old cemetery, please keep the location to yourself. The miners and their families endured so much and received so little in return. Leave them to their final peace.

Your imagination may need to work overtime as you wander, however, for man and weather have radically altered the land since 1879. Dumps are still visible on the slopes of Red Mountain (Mineral Hill), but avalanches and earthquake-triggered rockslides have obliterated most of the portals. You can find only remnants of a few cabins; the snows of a hundred winters have broken down their roofs and collapsed their walls. Most structures were torn down and hauled away, their timbers, lumber and shingles reused for building or cut for firewood. Some machinery was moved to other mining camps; scrap dealers salvaged the rest. Roadfill now covers the upper end of Mammoth City; the small quarry on the southwest slope of Panorama Dome (now sheltering a water tank) supplied that fill. Damming Lake Mary has raised its level about six feet, changed its shape (Franklin Buck described it as nearly round) and drowned its island. Its natural shoreline, partly marked by old stumps now in the lake, is under water.

To jog your imagination and ease yourself into a ghost-town mood, remember that mining then depended largely on the muscles of men and mules, amply assisted by dynamite and blasting powder. This reminds me to caution you that old dynamite can become unstable and extremely dangerous. Blasting caps too are dangerous; with metal jackets encasing their powder charge, they are actually mini-grenades. If you come upon either, do not touch or move them but report your find to the sheriff or the Forest Service. Other cautions. Keep your dogs, your children and yourself away from mine portals. Rotten timbers and open shafts can be fatal hazards. Respect the "No Trespassing" signs on the small mines that operate intermittently; they are private property. Last of all, remember that on federal land, laws prohibit the removal of all prehistoric and historic artifacts—anything made by man. Removing them makes cultural reconstruction impossible and leaves that much less for others to enjoy.

The Old Flume

From the town of Mammoth Lakes, drive west up Highway 203 to the stop light where 203 makes a right turn and leads to the ski slopes. Do not turn right but continue straight ahead (southwest). You are now on Lake Mary Road heading for the Lakes Basin. Just before the bridge at the first lakes, Twin Lakes, you will find a parking area on the right. Park, walk across the bridge, cross the road and walk up it a short ways until you find a trail leading through the aspen and paralleling the stream out of Twin Lakes. Following the trail that heads slightly uphill, you will soon find yourself crossing a ditch—the remains of the covered flume that curved around the hill, carrying water from the lakes to the Mammoth Mining Company's mill at Mill City. This flume was critical to the mill's operation, for its water turned the Knight wheel (see below) that provided all the power for the 40–stamp mill. Although a snowslide has destroyed one section of the flume and aspen and willow have overgrown others, you can walk a good part of the flume with no difficulty.

Pine City

From Twin Lakes continue up Lake Mary Road. Construction of this road in the 1930s obliterated portions of Pine City and Mammoth City, for at that time no one thought much about preserving historic sites. Extensive fill now gentles the grade coming up from Twin Lakes and covers the upper portion of the ravine between Panorama Dome and Red Mountain. This fill has buried the upper end of Mammoth City and Mammoth Avenue, part of the toll road and probably some cabin foundations. Construction also obliterated much of a water-powered arrastre, at the junction of the side road to Lake Mary's inlet.

The Mammoth Lakes Pack Outfit (on your right) marks the approximate site of the Pine City Feed and Livery Stable's corrals and pasture. This busy stable served the saddle trains that carried freight and passengers twice a week between Fresno Flats (Oakhurst) and Mammoth City. Beyond Pine City, the wagon road narrowed to a saddle trail that swung northwest, heading for Mammoth Pass. This Fresno Flats Toll Trail was the most direct route across the Sierra to the San Joaquin Valley foothills and to stage and rail connections for San Francisco.

North and south of the stable were the cabins of Pine City. As late as the 1920s, a dozen cabins dating from the early days still stood there. This is also the general locale of Old Charley's cabin and arrastre (see chapter five).

The Mammoth Consolidated Mine

Beyond the pack station, take the first paved road to the left. Through the trees you can glimpse Lake Mary, the favorite locale for dancing, boating and picnicking. Follow the signs to the upper end of Coldwater Campground. From the eastern edge of the parking area, a Forest Service interpretive trail leads to the Mammoth

Consolidated Mine, which started up in the 1920s and closed down in 1933. Although it has nothing to do with the early camps, it is a fine example of a small hard-rock mining operation of a later time—a time when gasoline engines, not water wheels, powered the mill machinery and trucks, not horses, transported people and supplies. The family of Arch Mahan donated the buildings and equipment to the town of Mammoth Lakes. The interpretive trail was dedicated in 1989. Bunkhouses, the Mahan cabin and enough of the machinery remain so that you can see how the mine operated. Note that the mill was at the mine, not three-quarters of a mile away like the Mammoth Company's mill.

Mammoth City and the Mammoth Mines

Return down the roads you just came. After passing the pack station, take the first road to the right, the historic Old Mammoth Road. Today's road follows the general course of the original wagon road from Mineral Park to Mammoth City and Pine City. Until the Lake Mary Road was completed in 1937, it was the only route to the lakes. In 1920 the wagon road was rerouted to gentler grades, to make it easier for automobiles to drive to the lakes and to old Tamarack Lodge on Twin Lakes and to old Wildyrie Lodge on Lake Mamie. Today's road approximates that 1920s road. Although grading and widening the present road undoubtedly destroyed much of the old road and foundations, you can still find short stretches of the old wagon road in the trees, parallel to today's road, although each year they become more overgrown and harder to discern.

As soon as you turn onto Old Mammoth Road, start looking on both sides of the road for excavations and foundations here and there among the pines. This is the upper end of Mammoth City, where a third of the town burned on 14 November 1880. Mammoth Avenue, the main street, now hidden by aspen, was off to your right near the portal of tunnel four. Driving on down the road, you may notice a bronze plaque erected by the Bodie chapter of E. Clampus Vitus, of which this author is a member. This organization consists of assorted folks who have two things in common:

the love of a good time and a desire to keep alive the history, especially the mining history, of California.

Across the road from the plaque, a path leads to the dump below the portal of the Mammoth Mining Company's tunnel four. Looking up the talus slope, you can see three higher dumps; each one marks the portal of a major working. For a spectacular view of all four portals (collapsed and buried under rockslides but still recognizable), walk up the slope of Panorama Dome on the north side of the road. Several trails go to the top of the dome; one starts near the upper end of the Old Mammoth road, near its junction with Lake Mary road. The dirt road to the water tank soon narrows to a trail that provides wonderful views of the old sites as it leads up Panorama Dome.

Mill City

As you continue down Old Mammoth Road, watch for more rock foundations scattered along the slope on your left—overgrown with a hundred years of shrubs but still recognizable. Stop briefly at the first broad turnout on your left, just as the road begins a horseshoe bend downhill to the right. Down in the pines, about a quarter mile north, was the company's stamp mill. Below, to your right, is the tramway cut. Standing here, you can see the distance and the steep grade between mine and mill that the ill-fated tramway had to traverse.

To reach the big flywheel, about all that remains of the mill, continue on down the road to a small white fence on the right that marks the grave of Mary Townsend (see chapter five). Park and look for a trail directly across the road. The trail is well defined all the way to the mill site. Watch your footing when you cross a small stream, for its bank can be slippery; stay on the trail, away from the private cabins adjacent to the mill.

Suddenly, when you break out of the trees into a small clearing, you come upon the huge old flywheel and the mill's stone foundations. It is hard to believe that everything else has vanished in little over a hundred years. Here water from the flume was forced through a nozzle, hitting the cups of the water wheel (see below) under high pressure and turning it at high speed. Belts and axles transferred the resulting power to the flywheel and, in turn, to the stamps and all the other machinery at the mill. You'll help preserve what little is left of the old mill if you resist the urge to climb on the rockwork behind the flywheel; the mortar is crumbling and the rocks are loose.

The Historic Knight Wheel

Continuing on down the road, you will pass through a timbered area known in the mining days as Mineral Park, site of an important sawmill. After the road flattens out near the meadows, passes a fire station and curves left, watch on your left for a small rusty-red building with a six-foot water wheel and belt-drive wheels in front of it. As noted in chapter fifteen, this is the third location for the historic Knight water wheel. Although it is often referred to as a Pelton wheel, this particular design is a Knight wheel, engineered to produce maximum power from water of high pressure but low volume.

Hauled by teams across the desert from Mojave to Mill City and installed at the Mammoth Company's mill in 1878, this historic water wheel powered the entire stamp mill whose ruins you just viewed. Around 1895 Dr. Doyle and his crew hauled it up to Mammoth City to run his smaller mill. Five or ten years later, Charlie Wildasinn sledded it down to the meadows to make electricity for his resort, the Wildasinn Hotel. In the 1920s it supplied electricity to Charlie Summers' hotel and boarding house known as Mammoth Camp. Now permanently retired, this small wheel has been at the heart of every chapter of Mammoth's early history.

T J Johnston

MINING TERMS

Adit: the specific term for the horizontal passage leading from the surface into a mine. Sometimes confused with the general term *tunnel* (see below).

Amalgamation: the process of separating gold or silver from crushed ore by mixing the ore with mercury. The resulting *amalgam* consists of mercury mixed with the metal. The mercury is recovered by distillation and then reused.

Amalgamator: the person who extracts metals from ore by adding small amounts of mercury during the milling process.

Arrastre: the Spanish word for a simple mining mill. The word was adopted by American miners and you may find it spelled *arastra*, *arrastra*, or *rastra*. A round rock structure for crushing ore. Heavy abrasive stones are dragged around an enclosed rock floor, breaking the ore into small pieces. Powered by a water wheel or by domestic animals such as burros or mules.

Casing rock: the rock that is on either side of a vein or ledge. Today called *wall rock*.

Crosscut: an underground passageway driven at right angles to an adit, drift, vein, etc.

Cyanidation: the process of extracting gold or silver from ore by dissolving the ore in an alkaline solution of sodium cyanide or calcium cyanide and precipitating the gold or silver from the solution.

District: an administrative area whose boundaries were determined by the miners who established it. A district, such as *Lake District*, may encompass several mining camps. Used in a geologic sense, may indicate a mineralized area, as a *lode district* or a *placer district*.

Double-jack (and single-jack) miner (according to Mark Twain):

> But the rock became more compact...and...shortly nothing could make an impression but blasting powder. That was the weariest work! One of us held the iron drill in its place and another would strike with an eight-pound sledge—it was like driving nails on a large scale. In the course of an hour or two the drill would reach a depth of two or three feet, making a hole a couple of inches in diameter. (1872)

A double-jack hammer was a two-handed sledge hammer; a single-jack hammer, a one-handed sledge. A double-jack miner was one who used a two-handed sledge, often with another miner holding the irons. Drilling and blasting, miners averaged around three feet a day, occasionally as much as five or six feet. Three feet was considered a good day's work.

A single-jack miner held a two-pound hammer (a four-pounder for dense rock) in one hand and the *iron* (the drill or chisel) in the other. The iron ranged from six inches, for starting the hole, up to two or three feet long. The single-jack miner might own his own hammers, but the irons usually belonged to the company. He would turn the irons in at night for resharpening and pick them up the next morning on his way into the mine.

Drift: a horizontal passageway parallel to a vein; also a connecting passageway between two shafts or chambers.

Dump: a pile of waste rock that has been removed from a mine, often confused with *tailings*.

Free gold: gold found in loose particles or nuggets.

Free milling: milling ore that contains free gold, which is easy to extract.

Freeze-out: a tactic used by key stockholders to force down the price of a mining stock (such as by failing to properly develop the mines) and then buy out smaller shareholders.

Grizzly: a large metal grate used for sizing ore. Often it would be shaken to facilitate the sorting process.

Hanging wall: the underside of the casing rock or wall rock, along a slanting vein.

Highgrade ore: ore that yields a large amount of a valuable metal. **To highgrade:** to steal rich ore.

Ledge, lead, lode: a fissure containing metallic ore; a vein.

Ore: a mineral or rock from which a valuable component, especially a metal, can be extracted at a profit.

Placer gold: free gold found in the sands and gravels deposited by streams and glaciers.

Powder: dynamite; also black powder, which was shipped in small wooden kegs and detonated by the keg.

Portal: horizontal entrance to a mine.

Quicksilver: old term for mercury.

Raise: within a mine, an opening driven upward, in contrast to a *shaft*. Also used as a verb, meaning *to excavate an opening upward*.

Shaft: an opening from the surface driven downward into a mine.

Stamp mill: a mill that crushes ore with heavy iron-covered pestles (stamps). Sometimes called a quartz mill. One stamp plus its accompanying mortar, called a *battery*, weighed several thousand pounds. A forty-stamp mill contained forty batteries. Gold was amalgamated on the *apron*, a sloping copper-covered platform below the battery.

Stope: an excavation within a mine made by mining ore—usually upward, in a series of steps—from a steeply inclined or vertical vein.

Tailings: the pile of crushed ore left after milling. Old tailings sometimes contained considerable gold or silver, for the crude milling processes of the time often extracted only a small portion of the valuable metals.

Talus: a sloping mass of rock debris, either on a hillside or at the base of a cliff.

Tunnel: strictly speaking, a horizontal corridor going *through* a mountain. In this book I use the term in the sense that the Lake District newspapers and miners used it—to identify which adit or level they were talking about. Often confused with *adit* (see above).

Value of gold: in 1848 the U.S. standard price for gold was $20.67/oz. However, in California, because there was no U.S. mint to enforce the standard, gold brought only $16/oz. and gold dust brought $10 to $12. After the San Francisco mint opened in 1854, California gold price conformed to the U.S. standard. The Carson City, Nevada, mint opened in 1870.

Waste: rock that is not profitable to mill or mine.

Winze: within a mine, a passageway driven downward.

GOODS FOR SALE, MAMMOTH CITY 1878–1880

Listed below is a representative list of goods that George Rowan, the largest retailer in Mammoth City, offered for sale. The categories, descriptions and wording are taken from ads in the *Mammoth City Times* and the *Mammoth City Herald*.

Boots and Shoes: nailed boots, mining boots, cloth shoes, calfskin boots and shoes for misses and children, etc.

Dry Goods: plaids, sheeting, shirting, muslins, percales, calicoes, shawls, quilted skirts, felt skirts, etc.

Fancy Goods: Toilet soaps, perfumes, ribbons, hair oil, pins, needles, thimbles, hair brushes, hair pins, accessories for sewing and embroidery, etc.

Groceries: butter, cheese, dried fruits, canned goods, crackers, coffee, tea, sugar, flour, corn meal, oat meal, graham flour, candy, vegetables, wines, liquors, beef, mutton, ham, bacon, sausage, lard, etc.

Hardware: miners' tools, can openers, cork screws, butcher knives, nails, nuts, bolts, washers, padlocks, door butts, hinges, hasps, stoves, gas pipes, guns, pistols, ammunition, Vulcan Blasting Powder, fuse, wallpaper, window glass, doors, shades, blinds, etc.

Lumber: products such as flooring, shingles, boards and battings were produced at the Mammoth Steam Sawmill Company in Mineral Park.

Stationery; picture books, pens, pen holders, diaries, ink, ink stands, copy books, blank books, pencils, etc.

Tinware: galvanized buckets, tin plates, custard pans, lunch buckets, dippers, nutmeg graters, dish pans, wagon oilers, camp stoves, fry pans, milk pans, etc.

Some merchants limited themselves to a small, specialized portion of the retail market. For example, on 24 March 1880 the *Herald* ran ads from P. A. Wagner & Co. and George Stevens side by side. Both advertised themselves as dealers in stoves, tinware and hardware; both were located on lower Mammoth Avenue. On the same page, George Rowan, with probably the largest stock of hardware and tinware, advertised similar goods. As the boom days faded, it was apparent that there were too many merchants with too much merchandise for too few customers. Listed below are goods advertised by some of the smaller merchants.

Cigars, Tobacco and Cigaritas (small cigars).

Clothing: men's ready-to-wear shirts, pants, coats. (Ready-to-wear was still a novelty, supplanting homemade clothing. During the Civil War, the need to outfit several hundred thousand men with uniforms was the impetus to rapidly expand the ready-to-wear industry.)

Drugs and Medicines: hair tonics, hair restorers, oils, pills, salves, bitters, cough medications, patent medicines, etc.

Furniture, Beds and Bedding: blankets, quilts, comforters, four-poster beds, etc. "the finest quality to be found on this coast."

Ladies Wear: beaver gloves, knit gloves, hose, scarves, handkerchiefs, etc. (Ladies ready-to-wear was beginning to appear in the larger cities, but in 1880 rural American women made their own and their children's clothing.)

Queensware and Glassware: tableware for sale by the piece, by the setting or as a service for six, eight, etc. Some merchants labeled their queensware *crockery*.

WORKS CITED

Primary Sources

Bodie Daily Free Press, March 1885.

Bodie Standard, 9 Nov. 1880, 21 Dec. 1881.

Bodie *Weekly Standard-News*, 1 Feb. and 8 March 1882.

Buck, Franklin. *A Yankee Trader in the Gold Rush: The Letters of Franklin A. Buck*. Boston: Houghton Mifflin, 1930.

Bridgeport (Calif.) *Chronicle-Union*, 5 and 28 May, 10 Sept. 1881, 8 Nov. 1884.

California State Mining Bureau. *California Gold Mill Practices*. 1895.

Candelaria (Nevada) *True Fissure*, 23 April 1881, reprinted from the San Francisco *Daily Exchange*.

Clemens, Samuel L. [Mark Twain]. *Roughing It*. Hartford: American Publ., 1872.

DeGroot, Henry. "Mono County." *Report 10, California State Mineralogist*. California State Mining Bureau, 1890.

Doyle, Helen MacKnight. *A Child Went Forth*. 1935. (Reprinted under the title *Doctor Nellie*. Mammoth Lakes: Genny Smith Books, 1983.)

Engineering & Mining Journal. New York: 1879–1881.

Forbes, George W. "Notes by the Way" (title of column varies). Los Angeles *Evening Express,* 14 and 22 Jan., 9 Feb. 1880.

"George Dodge" (obituary). Oakland *Daily Times,* 25 August 1881.

Hammond, John Hays. *The Autobiography of John Hays Hammond.* 2 vols. New York: Farrar and Rinehart, 1935.

Mammoth City Herald, 1879–1881.

Mammoth City Times, 1879–1880.

Mining and Scientific Press. San Francisco: 1878, 1885, 1895–1904. "California Mountain Road and Region" 30 April and "Mines of the High Sierra" 2 July 1904.

Pacific Coast Annual Mining Review and Stockledger. San Francisco: October 1878.

Rigg, Tom. See Reed, Adele 1982.

Ryan, John H. "Substance of a Report upon the Mammoth Mines." Typed report. San Francisco, 27 May 1902 with notes appended after 1930. Copy obtained from the late A. E. Beauregard.

Sacramento Daily Union, "Revival of a Deserted Mining Camp" 13 August 1885, as reprinted in the *Grass Valley Union.*

San Francisco *Daily Alta California,* "Mammoth" 5 June; 24 July 1879.

San Francisco *Daily Stock Report,* "Lake Mining District" 5 June 1878, as reported in the *Bodie Standard.*

San Francisco *Morning Call,* 3 Jan., 17 July, 2 Sept. 1880.

U.S. Bureau of the Census. *Tenth Census: 1880. California,* Vol. 6. 1883.

U.S. General Land Office. Unpublished field notes and claim maps, Lake Mining District, 1878 and later years. In the files of the Bureau of Land Management, Sacramento.

Wasson, Joseph. *Bodie and Esmeralda.* San Francisco: Mining and Scientific Press, 1878.

Whiting, H. A. "Mono County." *Eighth Annual Report of the State Mineralogist.* California State Mining Bureau, 1888.

Wright, J. W. A. *The Lost Cement Mine.* Mammoth Lakes: Genny Smith Books, 1984. (Reprinted from the San Francisco *Daily Evening Post* 8 Nov.–13 Dec. 1879.)

Secondary Sources

Chalfant, W. A. "Tales of the Pioneers." Bishop (Calif.) *Inyo Register* 26 Dec. 1935.

___. *Tales of the Pioneers.* Stanford: Stanford Univ. Press, 1942.

___. *Gold, Guns, & Ghost Towns.* Stanford: Stanford Univ. Press, 1947.

Hendricks, Geo. *The Bad Man of the West.* San Antonio: Naylor, 1942.

Nadeau, Remi. *Ghost Towns and Mining Camps of California.* Los Angeles: Ward Ritchie Press, 1965.

[Nadeau, Remi.] "Mammoth: Timberline Treasure." *Fortnight* 15 Sept. 1952.

Reed, Adele. *Old Mammoth.* Palo Alto: Genny Smith Books, 1982.

Rinehart, C. Dean and Donald C. Ross. *Geology and Mineral Deposits of the Mount Morrison Quadrangle Sierra Nevada, California.* U.S. Geological Survey Prof. Paper 385. Washington, 1964.

Shinn, Charles H. *Mining Camps, A Study in American Frontier Government.* New York: Scribner, 1884.

Smith, Genny. *The Mammoth Lakes Sierra.* Second ed., 1964. (Fifth edition published by Genny Smith Books, 1989.)

Interviews

Beauregard, Don. Vice-president of the Mammoth Lakes Mining Corp., which was incorporated July 1981.

Blackburn, Ralph. Born in 1878, a carpenter in Virginia City in the late 1890s. The author's maternal grandfather.

Nadeau, Remi. Author. Great-great-grandson and namesake of the eastern Sierra's most famous early freighter.

Roeser, Mary and Lou. Owner-operators of Sierra Meadows Equestrian Center and, since 1960, of the Mammoth Lakes Pack Outfit.

Smith, Genny. Publisher, editor and author of eastern Sierra books.

Willard, Beatrice and Stephen. Owner-operators of the Willard Studio, Mammoth Lakes, from 1924 until their deaths. Stephen, the shy master photographer, died in 1966; Bea in 1977.

INDEX

Forbes, George, 30, 35
Freight rates, 62, 65
Fresno Flats Saddle Train, 65–66, 151

Gold Mountain. *See* Mineral Hill
Gold rush, 2
Gold, price of, 128, 160. *See also* Ore
Good times, 87, 97–99

Hammond, John Hays, 119
Happy New Year, 96–97
Hard-rock mining, 4
Headlight Mine, 22, 23–24, 136
Highgrading, 129–130, 159

Knight water wheel, 16, 19, 46, 138, 140, 154, 155

Lake & Bodie Stage Line, 60, 85
Lake District, 13; differences from gold rush camps, 3, 87; location of, xiv–xvii, 45; 1879 map of, 14–15; organization & naming of, 8; residents of, 68–72; short-lived mining revivals, 6, 135–141
Lake Mary, xiv-xv, 40, 98–99, 131, 138, 150, 151
Lake Mining Review. *See* Newspapers
Library, 86
Lisbon Mine, 24, 136, 140
Lost Cement Mine, 1, 8

Mammoth City Herald, 106, 116.
See also Newspapers
Mammoth City Times, 106, 110.
See also Newspapers
Mammoth City, 1, 3, 16, 17, 20, 36–39, 136, 143, 144, 149, 152; company town, 5, 109–112; fire, 113–114; maps of, 14–15, 45, 94–95
Mammoth Consolidated Mine, 6, 141, 151–152
Mammoth Lakes Mining Corp., 6
Mammoth Mine, 20–24, 25, 26, 136, 140; elevation of portals, 21
Mammoth Mining Company, 11–31, 77; mill shutdown, 106; mining & milling practices, 124–127; possible causes of failure, 31, 119–130, 131–134; organization of, 12; production, 18, 121–122, 140; sale by sheriff, 117–118; stock prices, 25–26, 104–106. *See also* Flume; Flywheel; Stamp mill; Tunnel; Tramway
Mammoth Mountain. *See* Pumice Mountain
Mill City 36, 39, 144, 153
Mineral Hill, 8, 13, 20, 22, 24, 25, 26, 27, 149; geology of, 9–10; location of, xiv-xv, 45
Mineral Park, 34–36, 67, 137, 144
Miners' cabins, 37, 41, 52, 55, 56, 102, 103, 142, 143
Mining, risky nature of, 5
Mojave, 59, 61, 64, 65, 80

Monoville, 7
Monte Cristo Mine, ix, 6, 22, 24, 25, 136, 140

Nadeau, Remi (wagon freighter), 64–65, 73
Newspapers, local, 74–78, 79; spelling & grammar, xi

Old Charley. *See* Albright
Ore (gold and silver), 159; assays of, 23, 123, 140–141; estimates of, 18

Paiute Indians, 69
Pine City, 39–43, 67, 136, 137, 142, 144; location of, 40, 45, 151; tales of, 48–57
Politics, 88, 90
Population: of California, 3; of Lake District, 3–4, 67, 136. *See also* Census 1880
Portal, definition of, 20, 159
Prejudice, 3, 4, 69–70
Prostitution, 90
Pumice (Mammoth) Mountain, xiv-xv

Railroads, 59, 60, 64, 80
Red Mountain. *See* Mineral Hill
Ryan, John H., 138–139

Sawmills, 34, 35, 68, 117
School, 86, 114
Sherwin Grade, 62–65
Stamp mill, 16, 17, 18, 46, 124–127, 141, 159; dismantling of, 118; loss of boiler, 64–65, 136
Supplies, sources of, 38, 59–66

Temple of Folly, 82, 84, 104
Toll trails and toll roads, 14–15, 40–41, 62–66, 151
Townsend, Mary, 52–54
Tramway, 26–31, 131, 153
Transportation, 59–66, 85. *See also* Railroads
Trout, absence of, 82
Tunnels, 20–23, 153; definition of, 20, 160

Wages, 84, 129
Wagon roads, 41, 59, 152; to Benton & Bodie, 60–62; to Bishop Creek, 62–65; difficulties of locating, 66
Wagons, 61
Whiting, H. A., 10, 121
Winter of 1879–80, 92–93, 96, 101–102

About the Author

Gary Caldwell was six months old when he made his first trip to the Mammoth Lakes country. He has been summering in the Lakes Basin ever since, except for two years in military service that included a year in Vietnam as a company commander. His summer jobs included one as a trail guide with the Mammoth Lakes Pack Outfit.

Caldwell received his B.A. degree from Claremont McKenna College and his M.A. degree in history from the Claremont Graduate School. His master's thesis is titled *Mammoth City, 1877–1881*. Studies and field work in archaeology and post-graduate work in history at UC Riverside followed. In 1970 Caldwell joined the faculty of Mount San Jacinto College in Riverside County, California, where he teaches history and archaeology. He has participated in archaeological surveys and excavations of sites in the U.S., Mexico and Peru and regularly serves as an archaeological consultant to the Mammoth County Water District and to the U.S. Forest Service in Mammoth Lakes. In 1985 Caldwell conducted an archaeological field school to excavate a site in historic Pine City, one of the mining camps in Lake District.

About the Editor and Publisher

Genny Smith Books began publishing on eastern Sierra history and natural history in 1976. Titles include: *The Lost Cement Mine, Doctor Nellie, Earthquakes and Young Volcanoes along the Eastern Sierra Nevada* and *Old Mammoth*.

Genny Smith is a graduate of Reed College. She has been a Mammoth Lakes summer resident since 1957. She is co-author and editor of the two authoritative eastern Sierra guidebooks: *Mammoth Lakes Sierra* and *Deepest Valley*. Both have had numerous printings and editions; together they have sold over 75,000 copies.

Other Books on the Eastern Sierra
Edited and Published by Genny Smith

The Lost Cement Mine

James W. A. Wright. 1984, 120 pages, cloth and paper.

After you finish *Mammoth Gold,* you may want to know more about the events that led to discovery of the Mammoth mine. J. W. A. Wright, after a trip to Mammoth City and Monoville in 1879, wrote down the stories that were then raging about the legendary Lost Cement Mine. Tales of a reddish, rusty-looking cement, thickly spangled with flakes of purest gold, somewhere on the headwaters of the Owens River. Tales that ignited a frenzy of excitement and brought hundreds of men frantically searching every inch of Pumice Flat and the upper Owens. Tales that continue to lure prospectors even today.

Old Mammoth

Adele Reed. 1982, 194 pages, cloth and paper.

Stories and memories of Old Mammoth. Superb collection of sketch maps, documents and historic photographs.

Doctor Nellie: The Autobiography of Helen MacKnight Doyle

Foreword by Mary Austin. 1983, 364 pages, cloth only.

One of California's first women doctors writes vividly of frontier life in Owens Valley and its mining camps from 1887 to 1920.

Mammoth Lakes Sierra

Rinehart, Smith, Vestal & Willard. Fifth edition 1989, 224 pages, paper.

Best-selling road and trail guide to the magnificent mountains and adjacent valleys lying east of the Sierra Nevada crest.

New edition in progress and coming soon:

Deepest Valley: Guide to Owens Valley, Its Roadsides and Mountain Trails. Companion book to *Mammoth Lakes Sierra.*

For prices and mail order information ⊘

Mammoth Chapter, Friends of the Library, PO Box 1468, Mammoth Lakes, CA 93546

Dealers, write ⊘

Genny Smith Books, PO Box 1060, Mammoth Lakes, CA 93546

Colophon

Composed in Quark Express using Stone Serif and Stone Sans Serif Adobe fonts on a MacIntosh II Computer by The Live Oak Press, Palo Alto, California.
Pages output on Allied Linotype L-300 image-setters by Transgraphics, Inc., New Berlin, Wisconsin.
Printed web offset by Malloy Lithographing, Ann Arbor, Michigan, on 60 pound Glatfelter B-31